THE SECRETS
OF THE AVEBURY STONES

THE SECRETS
OF THE AVEBURY STONES

BRITAIN'S GREATEST MEGALITHIC TEMPLE

TERENCE MEADEN

SOUVENIR PRESS

First published 1999 by
Souvenir Press Ltd.,
43 Great Russell Street, London WC1B 3PA

ISBN 0 285 63501 8 (paperback)
ISBN 0 285 63502 6 (casebound)

Printed in Singapore

CONTENTS

ACKNOWLEDGEMENTS

The support and encouragement of Professor Ronald Hutton, University of Bristol, was much appreciated when I introduced him to the first carved heads and the enigmatic vulva marks at West Kennet long barrow and Avebury and explained the principle of the Sacred Marriage for the Avebury stones.

I must thank Alice Keens-Soper and Roger Finnigan, respectively Yorkshire TV producer and director, for the films on Stonehenge and Avebury made for Channel 4 and the Discovery Channel in 1998, and the National Trust at Avebury and English Heritage at Stonehenge for allowing us to perform the Sacred Marriage reconstructions.

My thanks, too, to Professor Radhakrishnan Praim Singh of Pennsylvania University for confirming aspects of inherent parallelism occasionally discernible between the Hindu religion and the Pre-Indo-European nature religion of the remote British and Irish Megalithic Age.

Dr Timothy Taylor, University of Bradford, helpfully supported the generalised Earth Mother hypothesis for the meaning of chambered and galleried long barrows at the time of making the Stonehenge/Avebury film when we were at Hetty Pegler's Tump in the Cotswolds.

Thanks also to Michael Pitts for welcoming the proposal that male-female fertility and the May Day solar alignment might explain the shapes, positions and functions of Stone 106 and the Obelisk.

My thanks to Dr Edwin C. Krupp, Los Angeles, and Professor Ian Hodder, Cambridge University, who provided good filmed support when treating, respectively, aspects of Earth Mother/Sky Father belief for the American Indians and female-deity belief for the Neolithic people of Catal Huyuk, Anatolia.

Lastly, I should like to thank the sculptress June Peel for verifying that a number of the heads at Avebury and West Kennet Long Barrow have carved features in addition to the natural ones.

TM

54 Frome Road, Bradford-on-Avon,
Wiltshire BA15 1LD.

1

SECRETS IN STONE

The early years of Avebury and the nature of the newest discoveries

Between 4,500 and 4,000 years ago the wonderful stone monuments of Avebury and Stonehenge were at the height of their glory. Constructed by neighbouring tribes thirty kilometres or nearly twenty miles apart on the chalk plains of Wiltshire, they were the world's finest temples of their age; and despite the heavy damage of recent centuries enough remains for us to marvel at the extraordinary efforts of the devoted men and women who built them as the focal sites of their culture.

Using sarsen stones dragged from the hills, Avebury's circles and avenues were built on a gigantic scale. The biggest surviving stone—the Swindon Diamond Stone at the North Entrance—weighs some 60 tons; and the biggest stone of all, whose dimensions were checked by the antiquarian William Stukeley in 1723, shortly before its destruction, weighed nearer 80 tons. This was the Obelisk, the tall centre-stone of the Southern Inner Circle.

At first sight Avebury's stones show few signs of carving. This contrasts with Stonehenge where it is obvious that the sarsen megaliths of the outer circle and the inner U-shaped sarsen feature, all of which came from the hills of Avebury, were carefully dressed. Because of this, and for other reasons too—like the startling beauty of the lintels high above the heads of the onlookers—Stonehenge has become the world's most famous prehistoric monument. Yet Avebury is bigger and more complex, and in many ways more fascinating and ultimately more satisfying.

Avebury and its neighbourhood are a major World Heritage site. An English Heritage Management Plan of the 1980s proclaims Avebury as 'represent[ing] the Henge monument *par excellence*, as the largest, most evolved and best preserved prehistoric temple of a type unique to Britain. Together with the associated sites and monuments [it] provide[s] a landscape without parallel in Britain or elsewhere and provide[s] an unrivalled demonstration of human achievement in prehistoric times.' Moreover, Avebury has an appeal which derives from its enormity of scale—proof of unfamiliar beliefs and lost skills from a faraway culture—and the plentiful puzzles posed by monuments close by, such as Silbury Hill, chambered long barrows, hilltop causewayed enclosures, and some lesser stone circles. Their many subtleties offer unexpected insights into the meaning of Avebury's art and architecture, much of which is revealed for the first time in this book.

* * *

The start of the Megalithic Age in southern Britain can be traced to the early part of the fourth millennium before the common era (written BCE on the universal time scale). By 3800 BCE, a thousand years or so before the first stones were erected at Avebury, scores of stone-chambered barrows had been constructed. The magnificent one at West Kennet was built around 3600 BCE, and its study has contributed much towards understanding the purpose of the megaliths of Avebury. The hilltop causewayed camp at Windmill Hill also came early in the Avebury story, and it, too, provides clues to the activities of the ancestors of the megalith-loving peoples.

The chronology of megalithic Avebury is unclear because so few radiocarbon dates exist—as Michael Pitts and Alasdair Whittle concluded in 1992—but enough is known to claim that within a century or two of the start of the third millennium, probably not later than 2800 BCE, Avebury's remarkable adventure began, and in the ensuing five centuries all the chief components were constructed. It can be argued that these labour-intensive achievements went hand in hand with the rise of a powerful leadership which benefited from the influence of organised religion and a well-loved belief system and mythology—possibly inspired in the early stages by the vision of some particularly charismatic figure.

The result was the most splendid constellation of ordered standing stones that the world has seen, together with Europe's highest artificial mound and the world's biggest ditch-and-banked stone circle. The end of the building programme in the late Neolithic era coincided roughly with the closure of the ageing chambered mounds and the start of the Beaker Period, at the same time heralding a thousand years of burial beneath round barrows. The power of Avebury had attained unprecedented heights, but a decline was to set in. By about 1500 BCE—the middle of the Bronze Age—Avebury was abandoned, together with the beliefs that had sustained it for so long. It was the same at Stonehenge and, as time passed, at all Britain's megalithic sites. Some cultural disaster had befallen the megalith-loving peoples.

Even so, the Avebury megaliths remained at peace and unharmed, except by frost and weather, for a further 2,500 years, respected but not understood by curious visitors and local farmers. Then, around 700–800 years ago, a community which had been living quietly inside and outside Avebury Henge for some five centuries came under the influence of condemnatory preachings of the Church, and centuries of wilful destruction followed.

At first, stone burial was the norm; but as time passed stone-breaking commenced and took its toll until it was stopped at Avebury in the nineteenth century, although at sites farther afield not until the middle of the twentieth century.

At last, in the 1930s, Avebury's fortunes turned. A rescue programme began, initiated by marmalade-millionaire Alexander Keiller who purchased part of Avebury village, pulled down buildings and began restoring the monument. Some megaliths were found safely hidden below ground and were re-erected, but others had been irretrievably smashed, their parts dispersed for ever. Keiller's restoration work in the period 1934–39 was exemplary, but it ended prematurely at the outbreak of the Second World War in 1939 and afterwards ill-health overtook him. Too unwell to continue, he died in 1955. More than anyone else during the twentieth century, he was responsible for the stone-studded Avebury that we admire today. Now, 60 years on, there is a fresh surge of interest as the stones yield more of their secrets.

The latest findings are of two kinds: *the first* is the rediscovery of the scheme, within the ritual of the Neolithic belief system, by which stones of Avebury's South and North Circles were assigned *solar-calendrical duties, the objective being fertility*. To achieve this, the concept was made visible by a policy of gender assignment. Alexander Keiller and Stuart Piggott spotted the inherent sexual possibilities of Avebury's megaliths when disinterring stones of the Kennet Avenue in 1934–36. Writing in *Antiquity* in 1936, they classified stones according to shape which they labelled 'Type A' and 'Type B'. Isobel Smith, in her book on Keiller's excavations at Avebury (1965), summarises the situation as follows:

Stones of *Type A* were defined as being much taller than their width, and having sides more or less parallel and vertical when erect; it was hesitantly suggested that the ancient Britons may have regarded such stones as male.

Type B stones were specified as being much broader, their breadth sometimes (but not necessarily) exceeding their height. Typical are squarish or rhomboidal stones, the most extreme of which are lozenge-shaped stones balanced upon a point. These were thought to be possibly female stones. Occasionally opposite types were paired together, as in the Kennet Avenue where pair numbers 13, 18, 26 and 32 are good examples.

One of several pairs of stones in the avenue which typifies the Type A and B stones defined by Alexander Keiller. Stone 13b is lozenge-shaped with a hint of a left-facing profile toward Avebury henge, while Stone 13a is a male-type pillar. Photographed at 12.30 p.m. BST, 11.30 a.m. GMT, 27 April.

In recent years there has been considerable progress in analysing ancient symbols, especially Neolithic ones. Comparisons can also be made with symbols from extant religions whose meanings and ancient origins are adequately understood. Thus, following traditional spiritual symbolism as acknowledged by hundreds of millions of Hindus and Tantrics over thousands of years, stones and images dominated by a simple isosceles triangle are always viewed as female.

On its own, the triangle is the Yoni Yantra or Kunti Yantra, because it symbolises the vulva and pubic zone by which it stands for the Great Mother as the source of all life. At the same time it is the sign of the original trinity—the triple goddess in her three ages of maiden, mother and wise woman. The lozenge symbol goes farther, for it is made up of two triangles base to base, in which the upward-pointing triangle can indicate the navel triangle—which is what it may do here.

In fact, there are places in the Avebury region where the downward-pointing triangle

Cup-mark 50mm (2ins) deep carved at the apex of a triangular sarsen stone weighing 31kg (68lb). It is one of three similar British Neolithic objects from near Avebury which hint at the spirit of Hindu/Tantric icons. Some of the cup-marks on stones and rocks at other Neolithic-Bronze Age sites may have a similar fertility significance.

has been found in conjunction with an artificially-carved vulvar hole or slit, a common symbol in Hindu India, both ancient and modern. Illustrated here is one of three Neolithic sarsen stones of portable size which I have found in the Avebury region. Each of them has the vulva defined by a pecked-out circular area. It is feasible that there may also be female significance in the round cup-marks found elsewhere in Britain. A different, but uncertain, possibility appears on damaged Stone 31 in the north-west quadrant of Avebury's outer circle, where a triangle apexed by a round hole might have been disfigured by villagers before they buried the stone.

At the time of Keiller's Windmill Hill excavations in the 1930s a chalk object was unearthed, carved in the shape of a lozenge and perforated at its centre, towards which grooves are directed (see *The Goddess of the Stones*, p. 136). In what may have served as a charm or votive object, present-day devotees of Tantric and Hindu goddesses would see intense female symbolism; so, too, could the worshippers of the Avebury region.

Related Neolithic lozenge-shaped objects found in the Avebury area are discussed in Chapter 15. Most are struck from flint stone, but one is made of oolite, the limestone rock imported from the Bradford-on-Avon/Bath/Wellow area, 30 kilometres (19 miles) to the west, and often used in Neolithic long barrows for dry-stone walling.

Near its centre a circular cup-mark was drilled in ancient times—further evidence that the symbolism of cup-marks relates to the female sex.

The circle is a well-known female symbol in the Tantric Hindu religion. Similarly, at Avebury, when devotees required a megalith to be feminine, instead of selecting lozenges they sometimes chose megaliths with a roughly circular outline (like Stone 105) or stones impressed with rings and U-shapes (as with Stone 4) or pitted with many holes.

The cup, circle and hole equate with the vulva as the Tantrics know well because they paint a vulvar circle on the wall at a wedding reception and add a central red dot (for the penis) as a gesture of good will for a fertile marriage. Other female symbols include vertical vulva-like grooves (as with Stone 106) or deep holes (Stone 32), great clefts (as with Stones 102 and 103), and vulvar-related holes which are total perforations through the rock (as with Avebury's Ring Stone). These and other aspects of gender assignment are discussed more fully in later chapters.

The second secret of the stones is even more subtle.

In ancient times, having positioned the stones in circles or avenues, or as coves, skilled artists set about creating what might be described as 'minimal sculpture'. For, of the undamaged standing stones which can be studied today, the majority bear traces of a nearly-invisible art-form, the result of a subtle sculptural technique which is difficult to spot unless one knows what to look for.

When studied closely *from particular angles*, regardless of the time of day, some of the stones reveal profiles of human heads or faces, or more rarely animal heads. But when the sun is out and shining at critical angles and at certain times of day, many more heads can be seen, usually one side only *and always with an eye*.

The megaliths were well selected and carefully positioned. In some cases it is possible that little or no sculpture was needed except for the addition of an eye or perhaps a mouth; in others, quite big areas of the surface were dressed, as possibly with Stone 26a in the Kennet Avenue. The sculptors generally took advantage of natural cracks, fissures, holes and hollows, which they sometimes extended. So on some stones one may suppose that the heads were entirely natural, while on others they were present only because sculptors had laboured to create them.

The only previous writer known to have touched on the subject of Avebury's heads is Paul Devereux (1992) who mentions heads or faces on half-a-dozen stones at the henge and along the Kennet Avenue, including the obvious Stones 35a and 37b. He wonders whether this could be evidence of a dreamtime era in which objects were invested with mythic attributes. Nonetheless he also says that most such 'faces and figures . . . clearly result from what could be described as a megalithic version of the Inkblot or Rorschach Test', caused by the viewer's own 'mental projection on to accidental ambiguous shapes'.

Some sceptics might wish to claim that all such likenesses result from chance fracturing, natural wear of the sarsen rocks, and the viewer's imagination. Such suspicions are easily dispelled, for if they were genuine, the numbers of right-facing and left-facing profiles would be roughly equal, which they are not.

Of the undamaged megaliths inside Avebury Henge which bear recognisable heads (which means the majority of them), left-facing heads number 50 as against nine right-facing ones. There are no examples within the henge of a right-facing head being unique to a stone. On the few stones where a right-facing profile has been found, one or more in left-profile are present too. What is more, because it is a common, near-universal rule in early symbolism that left-sidedness implies femininity and right-sidedness masculinity, this would give a gender-bias to these megaliths. In addition, there are over a dozen megaliths, some of which have no profiles or heads, which appear to be feminine either because of their shape or because they carry feminine symbols. Lastly there is the phenomenon of triplicity. Some stones have three heads—and when they come in threes the heads are always left-sided, implying female- or goddess-triplicity.

Of course it is important to avoid being misled by Rorschach-type occurrences (for which the left-right frequencies on average balance out), but the heads really are there, for all to see, and for everyone to check under the conditions described above. They are likely to be heads which the Neolithic worshippers knew too, and that is the ultimate criterion.

In total, when the 44 surviving megaliths inside the henge are sexed according to the given definitions, *43 turn out to be female and only one is truly male*! Every surviving megalith on the perimeters of the three stone circles is a female stone. And while megaliths along the Kennet Avenue and at West Kennet Long Barrow include some right-profile heads, it is left-sided or female heads which again predominate in a similar ratio. Lastly, where heads have been found on portable, carved stone objects, they have invariably been of the left-sided kind.

The left/right profile imbalance agrees with the theory, published in *The Goddess of the Stones* in 1991, that in the symbolic art of the Neolithic world left-handedness leads over right-handedness because of the higher devotion given to female deities than to male gods. In Neolithic religious scenarios left-handedness signifies the divine feminine, right-handedness the divine masculine, which means Goddess and God, Moon and Sun, or Earth Mother and Sky Father respectively. In *The Goddess of the Stones* the context was the interpretation of megalithic carvings in which spirals of either direction appear; in the present book we shall be assessing the significance of images seen in left or right profile. Identifying the implied sexuality of stones and their solar-calendrical properties helps to solve the fundamental problems of the meaning of Avebury—and Stonehenge as well.

Inside Avebury henge there used to be some 98 stones in the outer ring, and 27 and 29 in each of the inner rings. To these one can add the Obelisk and a minimum of 13 other stones associated with the South Circle, the three or four cove stones plus another

Stone 32, north-west quadrant. Instead of a female left-profile head on this stone, there are impressions of a female body. Photographed at 8 p.m. BST, 7 p.m. GMT, 19 June.

12 associated with the North Circle, and the Ring Stone. The total is at least 184 stones, probably more.

The Kennet Avenue is believed to have contained some 200 megaliths, and the Beckhampton Avenue a possibly similar number. If we add the 60 stones of the Sanctuary and the 12 for Falkner's Circle, the total exceeds 600 megaliths. Excluding fragments like Stones 73 and 209, only 81 remain in sight today: 44 inside the henge, 34 along Kennet Avenue, one at Falkner's Circle and two at Beckhampton.

If it had not been for the destruction wrought at various times in the Christian era, all the stones would be with us now—few of them damaged, even by frost and weather. One can only hope that a couple of dozen more may still be recovered from unexcavated areas, especially the eastern quadrants of the henge and the part of the Kennet Avenue approaching West Kennet Farm; and the sooner this is done the better. There is no doubt that when the Avebury villagers were demolishing megaliths, they were destroying art, and it was art of a rich and exceptional quality.

2

AVEBURY'S STORY
Origins and plans

The earliest evidence for settlement in the Avebury district is a series of house-floor sites with post-holes and hearths on Golden Ball Hill (SU 133 639). These were uncovered in 1997 by a University of Wales team from Cardiff, as reported in *British Archaeology*, and seem to date from around 4500 BCE, as the hunter-gatherer Mesolithic Age was ending. The biggest floor, about 15 × 10 metres (50 × 33 feet), consists of selected smooth flint pebbles. Tools typical of the Late Mesolithic and an absence of pottery imply a date prior to the Neolithic, the age when forests were being cleared at the start of Britain's agricultural period.

Close by are Knap Hill and Rybury Hill, while a few kilometres to the north, overlooking the plain upon which the megaliths of Avebury would rise, is Windmill Hill. On these summits were dug a type of causewayed enclosure—a simple earthwork made up of irregular concentric ditches with short gaps or access-passages left uncut in the sub-surface chalk. The one on Windmill Hill remained in use during the latter part of the fourth millennium (say from 3300 BCE onwards) and much of the third millennium. In his book on *Abury* (1743) William Stukeley said of Windmill hill: ''Tis a pretty round apex, the turf as soft as velvet. There is the sign of a very old camp cast up on one half of it but unfinished.'

The excavations of Alexander Keiller and H. St George Gray in the 1920s made Windmill Hill famous as the classic type-site for Neolithic causewayed camps or enclosures. Although their purpose is unknown, they are thought to have been seasonal meeting arenas with corral-like features of the sort that would be convenient at country fairs. Recently some of the bone deposits from a settlement site on Windmill Hill which *preceded* the causewayed-enclosure period have been dated to around 3700 BCE, predating the latter by 300–400 years.

Early long barrows of an earthen type include Horslip barrow on the southern side of Windmill Hill, South Street barrow between Avebury Trusloe and Beckhampton, and the long barrow which can be seen near the Beckhampton roundabout. An antler from a side ditch at Horslip has been dated to 4000 BCE, plus or minus 200 years. Datable material from the South Street barrow corresponds to the middle of the fourth millennium.

By 3600 BCE, perhaps earlier, stone-chambered long barrows were being built, their chambers constructed from massive sarsens dragged from the downs. This marks the start of Avebury's Megalithic Age within the Early Neolithic period. Among such barrows is the five-celled chambered barrow at West Kennet which was excavated and restored by Stuart Piggott in 1954 and 1955. Pottery studies and carbon-dating of bone deposits suggest that it remained in use for more than a thousand years, the oldest bones dating from about 3700–3500 BCE. A useful review of the many stone-chambered barrows constructed in the Avebury region was published by C. T. Barker in 1984.

Avebury's megaliths were raised during the third millennium. At some stage the chalk mound of Silbury Hill was built. The latest discussion on dating by Alasdair Whittle in 1997 has not resolved the problems of pinpointing its period of construction. The 28th century BCE was proposed by Richard Atkinson, the excavator who reached the interior of Silbury in 1968–70, but additional radiocarbon data have confused not clarified the issue. It is now thought that the mound could be three or four centuries younger. Silbury is more than a well-built high mound of quarried loose chalk stored securely within drum-like walls of chalk blocks, because at its centre is a lesser first-stage mound of turves around whose perimeter lies a primitive ring of sarsens—effectively a stone circle inside the hill. The significance of the curious ritual deposits was discussed by Michael Dames in 1976 and by myself in *The Goddess of the Stones* (1991).

The order of construction and the specific dates of the components of Avebury's megalithic phases have not been well defined either, but evidence suggests that some of the earliest elements, maybe starting about 2800 BCE, would have been the two 100-metre (328-foot) diameter rings of stone known as the North and South Circles. The former encircled a four-stone cove, the latter an 'obelisk'. A second cove 1,500 metres (1,640 yards) to the west at Beckhampton may well be about the same age.

Besides what has been learnt from careful twentieth-century excavations and restorations, much of what we know of Avebury's megaliths is due to the plans and descriptions of dedicated seventeenth- and eighteenth-century antiquarians. Without their aid the positions and shapes of several major missing megaliths would not be known now.

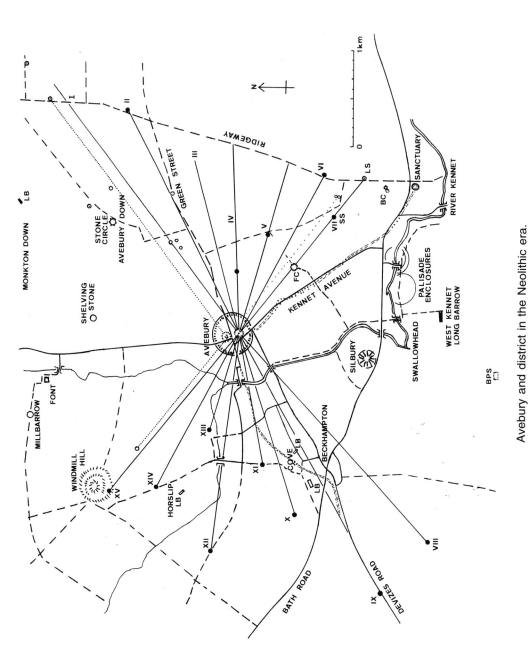

Avebury and district in the Neolithic era.

I to XV are lines extended outwards from 15 calendar stones of Avebury's South Circle, most of which intersect with known standing stones indicated by a black filled circle. Small open circles denote big sarsens now absent; circles with a dot indicate some of the major sarsens still present. FC = Falkner's Circle. BC = barrow circles. SS = Stukeley's Stones. LS = white lozenge

The first of these was the Wiltshire intellectual John Aubrey (born 12 March 1626, near Kington St Michael, Chippenham; died June 1697) who encountered Avebury by chance in January 1649 in the course of a hunting expedition. He returned in the 1650s and made the first plans of the monument. As he did so, stones were disappearing, for it was the Puritan Revolution, and an evangelical meeting-house (founded in 1660 by John Baker) was going up inside the arc of Avebury's South Circle, concerning which William Stukeley specifically stated (in 1723) that a stone 'in the garden was destroyed to build the meeting house'.

Although huge numbers of megaliths had vanished before John Aubrey's time, he greatly admired those remaining, and wrote in his *Monumenta Britannica* that 'Avebury . . . did as much excel Stonehenge, as a cathedral does a parish church'. He recorded a downside too. From the villagers he learnt how the big stones were being broken into pieces, having been fractured by fire and water.

'Make a fire on that line of the stone, where you would have it crack; and after the stone is well heated, draw a line with cold water, & immediately give it a knock with a Smyths sledge [a hammer], and it will break, like the Collets [circular moulds] at the Glass house.' Years later, William Stukeley heard the same, and added that the stone was toppled over a straw-filled pit and the straw set alight.

About 1662 John Aubrey informed the physician Dr Walter Charleton of Avebury's immense stones, following which Dr Charleton—also a Westcountryman (born 1620 in Shepton Mallet, Somerset; died 1707)—drew a useful plan too. Together with King Charles II and his brother (the future James II) Aubrey and Charleton visited Avebury in 1663, probably in the spring. On 8 July, 1663, there was a presentation at the Royal Society in London in which the 'Stone-Antiquity of Avebury' was discussed. The book by Peter Ucko, Michael Hunter, Alan Clark and Andrew David (1991) provides excellent detail about the earliest periods of antiquarian research at Avebury.

Later came Dr William Stukeley (born at Holbeach, Lincolnshire, 1687; died 3 March, 1765). He ranks among early antiquarians as Britain's most observant field archaeologist, for he delighted in examining ancient curiosities, especially during the period 1719 to 1725, but his natural intelligence was hindered by his desire to explain the prehistory of Britain, Avebury and Stonehenge on the basis of Biblical ramblings. Stukeley visited Avebury every year from 1719 to 1724, making competent sketches, plans and notes which are of enormous value today.

When John Aubrey and Walter Charleton arrived at Avebury, a dozen of the 29 megaliths making up the perimeter of the South Circle were present, either standing or fallen. A huge central stone, known since Stukeley's time as the Obelisk, lay prone. The series of six quite small megaliths nearby (Stones iii to viii)—part of the puzzling Z-setting dug up by Alexander Keiller in 1939—were not then visible; mediaeval villagers had concealed them below ground.

At least 16 perimeter stones of the North Circle were present in 1663, as well as

Megalith destruction with fire and sledgehammers, as drawn by William Stukeley.

others including what appear to be the four stones of a central feature which William Stukeley in the 1720s said 'the old Britons call a cove'. By then, two cove stones remained, a third having been removed a few years earlier. Stukeley spotted that the cove 'opens pretty exactly north-east, as at Stonehenge'. Indeed, as at Stonehenge, the cove faces the summer-solstice sunrise.

These stone circles lie within the henge which is outlined by a deep circular trench with an external high bank broken by four entrance causeways at the cardinal points. The ditch (called the dyke by the locals) was dug to an average depth of nine metres (30 feet) but deepened to 10–11 metres (33–36 feet) by the entrances. Its excavation involved the removal of 90,000 cubic metres (3.2 million cubic feet) of chalk. The height of the bank above the ground used to be a level 6.5 metres or 18 feet. The circumference of the ditch is 1,350 metres (4,440 feet), or more than four-fifths of a mile. The area enclosed is 11½ hectares or 28½ acres.

The digging of the dyke and the raising of the Great Stone Circle were probably planned together, the latter preceding the former by a moderately short interval. All but one of the Great Circle stones for which information is known had been raised from the inside. Excavation facts are given by Isobel Smith (1965) in the official report of Alexander Keiller's excavations. The initial digging was into hard Middle Chalk. Deeper into the dyke softer and older Lower Chalk was encountered. Keiller and Piggott found that blocks of Lower Chalk had been used as packing material at the bases of stones of the Z-setting and one of the nearer stones of the Kennet Avenue (Stone 9b), showing that these stones were erected late in the stone-raising period over 4,000 years ago.

The 2½ kilometre (1½ mile) long Kennet Avenue ends at a monument which used to consist of two concentric stone circles, made up of smaller than average megaliths— 1.5 metres (5 feet) high or less. Stukeley called this the Sanctuary or 'The Temple on Overton Hill'. It was almost entirely destroyed during 1723 and 1724. Early in its history the Sanctuary had consisted of concentric rings of posts which had been contemporary with part of Avebury's megalithic building-period, before their replacement by two concentric circles of stone around 2500 BCE plus or minus a century according to Joshua Pollard. At some stage, more likely early in the period, a second stone avenue was almost certainly built, linking the cove at Beckhampton with the Avebury circles and its cove, and towards the end of the stone-building era two large timber-palisaded enclosures were built at West Kennet.

Judging largely by the finds and locations of pottery types and the limited knowledge gained from carbon-dating, the monuments were built over a period spanning the centuries from 2800 to 2300 or 2100 BCE. Of course, the Avebury operations cannot be considered without some reference to events at Stonehenge. There was a prolonged period when sarsens were being erected at Stonehenge, having been dragged from the Avebury Hills. This could not have happened without the authority and consent of the Avebury peoples. Using the new dating evidence provided by Rosamund Cleal and her colleagues in the English Heritage Stonehenge book, a section of the outer trilithon circle at Stonehenge has acquired a relatively secure date centred around 2400 BCE, from which it seems likely that the inner trilithons had an earlier date of say 2450 or 2500. This suggests that Avebury's principal megalithic circles which consist of 'rude, unhewn rocks' (as early writers put it) had been completed by then; and that as work continued at Stonehenge the people of the Avebury district finished off their monuments (Z-setting, Ring Stone, one or maybe both avenues, Silbury Hill and the West Kennet palisaded enclosures) and quietly worked on their secret sculptures, refining the stones in a way that outsiders would not know.

* * *

Compared with the great number of wild theories that have been directed at Stonehenge over so many centuries, the scale of speculation about Avebury's origins has been more limited.

In Camden's *Britannia*, 1695 edition (p. 637), it is recorded that John Aubrey suspected the Avebury Circles to be Temples of the Druids. Elsewhere this proposal was given the status of a 'probability', after which, when writing generally about prehistoric monuments, he said, 'I now think it a surer way to say, Monuments erected by the Britains'.

Walter Charleton, who enjoyed a long friendship with the Danish academic Olaus Worm, came to regard Avebury as 'a Monument of some Danish King'—as he did Stonehenge.

Thomas Twining, the vicar of Charlton in the nearby Pewsey Vale, published a pamphlet in 1723 saying—despite the lack of evidence in its favour—that Avebury was the 'Remains of a Roman Work', a temple to the god Terminus. He therefore called the Avebury temple Cunetium (after the river, as the Romans had done for their settlement Cunetio at Marlborough).

William Stukeley was next to publicise a theory about Avebury, and his is the best known. His 1743 proposal was comprehensive for the period, but wrong. Before then, his timely field work in the period 1719 to 1724 began and ended with careful plans, measurements, sketches, and detailed accounts of the earthwork, megaliths, the eighteenth-century village, and the surrounding prehistoric monuments. Early in this period the South Circle bore the appellation Solar Temple, the North Circle was called Lunar Temple, and the Temple on Overton Hill was named the Temple of Ertha, but the words Solar, Lunar and Ertha (also spelt Eartha) were struck out in 1724. But when his book *Abury* appeared twenty years afterwards it had more in it than worthy archaeology, for there was page after page of blithe invention about his Druidic insights into the ancient Britons and their fabled ancestors. The Beckhampton and Kennet Avenues were reshaped into more gentle curves than reality warranted in order to produce an easy serpentine appearance which better conformed with his Trinity theory of 'a snake proceeding from a circle' as 'the eternal procession of the Son [i.e. Christ] . . .' The Avebury stones were transformed into a 'Dracontium' or Serpent Temple, in which the circle stood for 'god's existence' traversed by a serpent symbolising 'his creative power'.

Stukeley, by now a country vicar, in his determination to designate via misguided patriotism the British Druids as inheritors of the Christian patriarchal religion, idealised them as the noble priests of 'the ancient and true religion'. In this way, Avebury having become a serpent-temple, the Beckhampton Avenue was identified as the tail of the serpent whose body, after embracing the Avebury circles, followed the Kennet Avenue to the snake's head at the Sanctuary on Overton or Kennet Hill.

(Opposite page) Part of William Stukeley's great map of the Avebury Temple drawn in 1724, showing the North and South Circles, and the positions of the Cove, the Obelisk, the Ring Stone, and a section of the great circle.

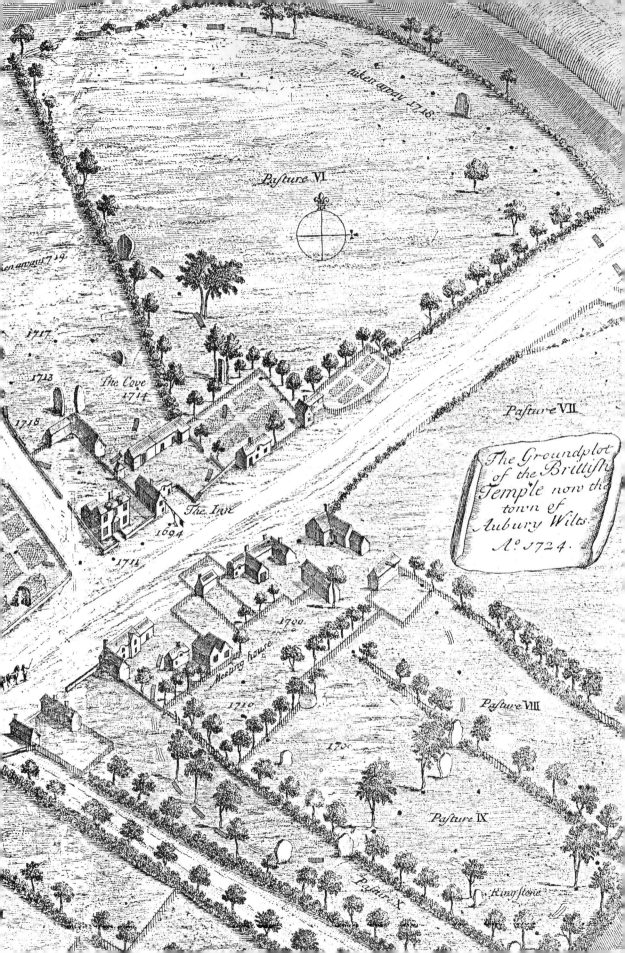

Pasture VI

taken away 1718

taken away 1719

1717

1713

The Cove
1714

1718

The Inn

1694

1711

Pasture VII

The Groundplot
of the Brittish
Temple now the
town of
Aubury Wilts.
A° 1724.

1700

Meeting house

1710

1700

Pasture VIII

Pasture IX

Kingstone

Over a century later, in 1860, James Fergusson saw Avebury as 'a vast grave-yard', in answer to which Alfred Charles Smith did enough digging in 1865 to demonstrate that it was not (Smith, 1867). Several other unlikely guesses as to the origins of Avebury were reviewed by William Long in 1858.

Even so, as late as 1928 O. G. S. Crawford (editor of *Antiquity*) still thought that 'the purpose was probably sepulchral. We may imagine that the Cove originally contained an interment—its arrangement when perfect recalls the burial-chambers of Brittany and Cornwall.'

Alexander Keiller and Stuart Piggott avoided theorising beyond suggesting a possible fertility significance for the stones. Dr Isobel Smith who prepared the archaeological report of their excavations discusses this briefly (1965) and concludes: 'If the [Type] A and B stones in the Circles and Avenue do indeed represent male and female symbols, the implication must be that the monuments were dedicated to a fertility cult.' How right she was!

Michael Dames in 1977 used an imaginative calendrical-festival approach and knowledge of folklore to present his visionary ideas, which added to Stukeley's dream scheme for Avebury and the avenues. Despite unwarranted and ambitious speculation, his study raised some interesting points, not least the general fertility aspect in the presence of the Earth Mother or Goddess.

Dr H. A. W. Burl takes an opposite viewpoint. He speculates that the celebration of death and the placation of ancestral spirits (funerary miming, as Peter Ucko words it) was the motivation for much of the effort that went into Avebury's monumental megalithic construction (Burl, 1979). He wrongly claims that the North Circle Cove approximates to the extreme northerly moonrise (which it does not because it faces the summer solstice sunrise) but he is right to say that the Beckhampton Cove may have been intended to face the winter solstice sunrise. Although the extreme northerly moonrise happens no more than once every 18 years, he suggests that the purpose of Avebury was nocturnal ceremonial marching carrying bones, which started at Beckhampton in the dead of winter and terminated at the North Circle Cove where the bones were deposited (Burl, 1988).

By contrast, the present book agrees with the idea of stone-fertility symbolism as proposed by Isobel Smith, Alexander Keiller and Stuart Piggott, but goes much further and provides a wealth of evidence hinting at the nature of the fertility cult in rediscovering the solar-calendrical devices built into the stone settings. Above all, there seem to be signs of a belief in the fertility deities—Earth Mother and Sky Father—which would have played a major role in the pagan-belief system of the Megalithic era.

All in all, the evidence of the stones tells us that a large, well-fed population and committed workforce must have been available in order to start, and complete centuries later, such an ambitious undertaking. Even supposing that much of the work was done at agriculturally slack times of the year, during the long periods when people

View southwards across the south-western quadrant at Avebury. In the distance megaliths of the Kennet Avenue are visible. Photograph taken at 5.30 a.m. BST on 21 June.

were shifting stones they were unable to help with the farmwork while requiring a constant and adequate supply of food.

Isobel Smith (1965) commented on the 'flourishing and prosperous society' that must have been necessary to carry out such an enormous and lengthy project. She said 'a high degree of social coherence is implicit in the planning and execution of these prodigious undertakings, presumably under the direction of a priestly hierarchy.'

She is right; and this leaves little or no room for planning and leadership by drug-taking shamans—a point which applies just as well to Stonehenge for which this unlikely proposal has recently been aired.

3

MAY DAY MARRIAGE
The Obelisk and its function

At the centre of the South Circle was Avebury's biggest stone, a gigantic 80-ton sarsen known as the *Obelisk*. A famous sketch was made by Dr William Stukeley on 10 July, 1723. Conscious of the stone's importance, he noted its dimensions, which useful piece of foresight has allowed its mass to be calculated. On page 24 of his book *Abury* Dr Stukeley wrote:

'The central obelisk of this temple is of a circular form at base, of a vast bulk, 21 feet long and 8 feet 9 inches diameter; when standing, higher than the rest. This is what the scripture calls a pillar, or standing image, Levit. xxvi.1. These works, erected in the land of Canaan by the same people . . . were ordered to be demolished by the Israelites, because at that time perverted to idolatry.'

Sixty years earlier John Aubrey and Walter Charleton gazed upon this stone. On the 1663 map Charleton wrote that it was 'the greatest stone of all, in the Centre of the lesser Circle'. As with other megaliths on Aubrey's and Charleton's plans, no sign is given to indicate whether stones were upright or fallen, but Charleton's observation may imply that this 'greatest stone of all' was then standing. Whatever the truth, by the time Stukeley saw it, it lay upon the ground.

Through the centuries the Christian Church had issued many edicts to encourage the disposal of stones that were sacred to the old religion. One such edict was proclaimed at the Council of Nantes about the year 896, and a part was reproduced by Isobel Smith in her account of the Keiller excavations (1965). Even long after

In this drawing of 1723 William Stukeley is seen standing by the fallen Obelisk. At the
far left are Stones 125 and 126. Farthest away in the centre are Stones 97, 98 and 1.
In front of 97 and 98 is the Ring Stone and in the middle of the picture Stone 101 is
recognisable. Stone 102 lies fallen to the right and 103 is standing. At the extreme right
lie Stones 105, 106 and 107. The remaining megalith, centre right, is probably Z-stone ix.

Christianisation, many country people retained a lasting faith in the ability of particular stones to promote fertility and good health, for which reasons at least some church-
going fundamentalists seem to have resolved to outlaw the megaliths. Gradually, the
people's acceptance of and affection for their ancient stones diminished until some
energetic inhabitant, more determined than the rest, took it upon himself to topple and
destroy them. Avebury's sarsens were probably under attack from the fourteenth
century onwards, and desecration may have begun long before. By the late sixteenth
century evangelists travelling through Wiltshire were spreading their own messages,
following which the people of Avebury built a meeting-house in 1660, and chose to
locate it close to the Obelisk inside the perimeter of the South Circle.

As the Puritan Revolution rolled on, Europe's megalithic heritage, having been under
attack for centuries, was disappearing faster than ever; when it came to stone circles,
the first stones to go were often the iconic centre stones, some of them phallic.

So Avebury's very masculine megalith—the Obelisk—was tumbled down, most likely in the century preceding Dr Stukeley's visits, and disposed of a few years after his last tour in 1724. Stukeley pointedly remarked that because the shape of the stone's base ensured good stability it could hardly have fallen without human aid. Alas, the Obelisk is no more, but the meeting-house remains—restored as recently as 1990 and 1998.

Following the excavation and reconstruction work of Alexander Keiller and Stuart Piggott it was estimated that the megaliths of the South Circle once numbered 29.

In assigning numbers to the stones, whether present or missing, I have followed the system originated by O. G. S. Crawford and used in Isobel Smith's report on Alexander Keiller's work. Thus the four South Circle stones shown standing in Stukeley's sketches are identified as numbers 101, 103, 125 and 126; while those which he recorded as present but fallen included 102, 105, 106, 107 and 110. Number 113 would have been the stone whose pieces, according to Stukeley, were used in the construction of the meeting-house.

All except 101, 102, 103, 105 and 106 on the western side of the ring are now gone, and it is these, following Keiller's reconstruction in 1939, which remain for us to admire. A few other South Circle stones may still be recovered if they lie safely buried beneath the turf of the eastern arc which Keiller never explored.

It is fortunate that *Stone 106* survives, because it is one of Avebury's most astonishing megaliths, thanks to the vulva-like impression on its inner face. Whether or not the groove is wholly natural is debatable, but that is not an issue. The point is that this most female of stones was chosen to occupy a special location facing the male Obelisk Stone on a May Day bearing, and that this was almost certainly done because of its explicit femininity. Knowing why blazes the trail to solving the iconography of Avebury.

The facts of alignment are exact and testable.

Vulva Stone 106 is aligned precisely with both the phallic Obelisk and the sunrise for the early summer May Festival which used to be observed everywhere in Britain. The bearing of 62½ degrees east of north corresponds to the modern calendar-date of 8 May when the sun appears over the Avebury Hills a mile away. At this moment the rays of the sun cast the phallic shadow of the Obelisk upon the Vulva Stone in a deliberate alignment which bears witness to the seasonal importance of the May Festival 4,500 years ago. Because the relative inclination of the ecliptic is forever changing, the sunrise bearing in Neolithic times of 62½ degrees would have occurred on 6 or 7 May which is the 47th day or midway date between the equinox and the midsummer festival, and regarded by many early communities as the start of summer.

This cosmic union of the stones, caused by the rising sun, expresses in visual terms the idea of fertility that underlies the universal rite of the *Marriage of the Gods*. It is a dramatic device. Such a spectacle could have been witnessed by expectant crowds waiting on the high western bank of the circular earthwork. Even today this is a good

Stone 106 with its prominent vulva mark. It is sited on the perimeter of the South
Inner Circle in the Early May sunrise position relative to the male Obelisk. The consequence
is that on May Day the long shadow of the Obelisk unites the two megaliths as if in
Sacred Marriage.

place to stand, for it lessens the effect of the trees which now interfere with a direct view to the horizon.

Recalling the creation myths known to have been prevalent throughout the ancient world, it may be argued that this way of expressing the Divine Marriage reveals a primordial belief at Avebury in the basic myth by which Sky God and Earth Goddess, or Sky Father and Earth Mother, mated at the beginning of time. By arranging this shadow-based, cosmic scheme as an annual happening, the Avebury people were reassuring themselves of the future success and prosperity of their hopefully fertile but uncertain world.

In much later Celtic, Teutonic, Norse and Anglo-Saxon times the sun seems to have been feminine, but during the Neolithic and Early Bronze Age periods—until that unexplained hiatus which drove the worshippers from ancestral Avebury and Stonehenge and brought the Megalithic Age to an end—the mounting evidence suggests that the sun was masculine, and that the religion included a Sky Father. The sun was visibly an inseminator (Eliade, 1958), sending its first morning rays into the wombs of megalithic temples and chambered barrows such as Maeshowe (Mackie, 1998), Newgrange, Stonehenge and Stoney Littleton (Meaden, 1992, 1997). The American Indians shared this belief and viewed the marital union of sun and earth as the mating of Sky Father and Earth Mother. The intervention of a phallic-type shadow, caused by the light of the rising sun, signifies a more complex mythology, which was similar at both Avebury and Stonehenge.

In the absence of the Obelisk the shadow spectacle can no longer be enjoyed, but it was reconstructed for a single day on Friday, 8 May, 1998 by myself and Yorkshire Television's film-makers headed by Alice Keens-Soper and Roger Finnigan. On this occasion a replacement for the Obelisk was devised in the form of a cloth-covered tower, and the film was broadcast to millions of viewers at the end of 1998.

At *Stonehenge* a similar May-Festival date-indicator was built into the Station Stones of the monument, as Astronomer-Royal Norman Lockyer discovered a century ago. Viewed from the centre of Stonehenge the 7th May sun (modern calendar) can be seen *setting* over Station Stone 93. This would allow the tribal skywatcher to announce that the May Festival could begin and that May Morning would be on the morrow, the 8th. Similar Beltane-related alignments exist at megalithic sites countrywide, which goes to show how widespread and long-held an interest in this Start-of-Summer Festival used to be.

I myself made the May-alignment discoveries at Avebury's South Circle in April-May 1996. Two years later, when walking the prehistoric Ridgeway which separates Avebury Down from Upper Overton Down, I came upon a rhomboid, triangular-topped megalith along whose middle a vulva had been pecked in ancient times. Having established its national grid co-ordinates (as SU 1266 7118), I checked the bearing from the Obelisk and found it to be again that of the May Festival, at 62½ degrees east of north. This means that the vulva stone on the hill had been positioned to align with

In this reconstruction the Obelisk (out of picture, to the left) is casting a phallic shadow on to the vulva mark of Stone 106 of the Southern Circle. The near circular outline of Stone 105 can be seen left of centre, while Z-stone vi is in the centre of the picture. In order that part of Stone 106 may be seen for the purpose of photography the line of the shadow has been slightly offset, which is equivalent to sunrise one or two days after true May Day. On May Day the shadow caused by the rising sun shining on the Obelisk aligns exactly with Female Stone 106.

the South Circle Vulva Stone 106 and the Obelisk, as well as the missing South Circle Stone 121.

This linear group had been planned about 4,000–4,500 years ago by South Circle worshippers. A distinctive stone was placed on the hill to define the spot over which the sun rose when viewed from Avebury on the morning of the May Festival; and the same bearing is reached again at the beginning of August—the occasion of the First Fruits Festival. Despite its distance from Avebury the vulvar hill-stone was a part of the South Circle complex. While its function is not yet known, it was certainly a marker stone; for instance, it marks the place where a beacon could have been lit, as if to 'rekindle the sun', in the event of an overcast night sky.

This is the fundamental Marriage-of-the-Gods drama which takes place at Avebury's May-Morning sunrise. The function of the male Obelisk was to play a role in a solar-earth connection between sun and a female perimeter stone of the South Circle. How many other stones might there be which function similarly on other dates of the year?

4

SHRINE OF THE GODDESS

The Calendar Stones of
the South Circle

My next step was to establish whether calendrical roles had been devised for other South Circle megaliths, and whether an outer series of stones had been set in place for them as well. The idea that the Sacred Marriage of the Gods was the fertility motive for the design plan of the South Circle enabled me to formulate *a set of predictions which could be tested*. So the search began, and the answers, while still incomplete thanks to the removal or destruction of stones over the centuries, look like ending up positively.

Only five megaliths of the South Circle remain, but the positions of others are known by their empty stone-holes and concrete markers. (See plan, p. 40.) Of the 29 original stones there were eight in a western arc and seven in an eastern arc whose positions, relative to the Obelisk, physically correspond to the rising or setting of the sun. They are numbered 105 to 112 and 120 to 126. All fifteen could have served in a Sacred Marriage context to define dates for the Avebury people's festivals. To what extent can this be confirmed by studying the stones near and far?

After female Stone 106, the next megalith to investigate is its neighbour, *Stone 105*. In the context of the fertility beliefs thought to have been held by the Avebury peoples, this is another womanly stone whose femininity arises from its near-circular outline.

In the custom of the Hindus, Tantrics and others whose traditions provide a symbolic link between the circle and the yoni or vulva, it offers the imagery of the genital circle. What is more, Stone 105 aligns with the Obelisk, Stone 120, and midsummer sunrise over Hackpen Hill. Therefore, just as the rising sun of 8 May casts the shadow of the Obelisk upon Stone 106, so the sun of 21 June comes over the hill and throws the shadow of the Obelisk upon the round female Stone 105.

In this way the stones were attuned to the Marriage of the Gods at the Midsummer Festival—perhaps imbued with their divine nature; and as it is a fact of astronomy that the directions of midsummer sunrise and midwinter sunset are directly opposite one another, so for the same alignment the setting sun of 21 December casts the shadow of the high Obelisk the opposite way, upon *Stone 120*, indicating that the Marriage was now an evening event instead.

If we look at the May-sunrise alignment of the Obelisk and Stone 106 from the

The nearly-circular Stone 105 of the South Circle. The stone faces the Obelisk in the direction of midsummer sunrise. Its outward side, shown here, is towards the midwinter sunset. This photograph was taken at 11.15 a.m. GMT, on 11 November.

opposite viewpoint, the same applies. In a sunset scenario the Obelisk and *Stone 121* are united at the beginning of November and the beginning of February.

Because Stones 105 and 106 are still in place, it is easy to confirm these alignments in relation to the Obelisk's concrete substitute, for instance by standing on the western bank of the henge to view the sunrises. Or else one can stand in front of the Obelisk and watch the sun set behind Stone 106 at Hallowe'en and at the start of February, or watch the midwinter sun set behind Stone 105. Paul Devereux mentions the midwinter sunset at Stone 105 while adding that 'this is probably fortuitous' (1992). However, it *is* part of the plan.

Four stones of the South Circle therefore provide calendar dates while performing what I believe the Avebury people would have seen as a Sacred Marriage—the known female Stones 105 and 106, and the inferred female Stones 120 and 121. How many others of the fifteen sarsens can be shown to have bearings which relate to dates on the solar calendar? And as with Stone 106 for which a related female stone has been found beyond Avebury's chalk walls, can a set of outer megaliths be found for all fifteen?

Besides searching on the hills and downs, I consulted large-scale maps and archival records. The fifteen principal extra-mural stones I sought are labelled with Roman numerals I to XV; among them is the vulvar stone on the Ridgeway which is now called *Outer Stone II.* For some important directions more than one stone may have been set up, one near the henge (not necessarily in sight from the Obelisk but having some sacred or other useful function), another on a hill-crest. The map on p. 12 summarises the results of this research.

Although they are known to have definitely existed, some Outer Stones have vanished without trace, like the equinoctial Stone IV (bearing 89 degrees east of north, same as South Circle Stone 123), and Stone V (bearing 107 degrees east of north, corresponding to Stone 124). Their exact locations are recorded in the archaeology department of the Wiltshire County Records Office where they are described as 'large sarsens' lately gone missing (that is, some 50 years ago now) before they could be assigned Ancient Monument numbers.

Outer Stones VIII (midwinter sunset), IX (SU 0702 6837, early November and early February sunsets), XV (midsummer sunset), X (bearing of 73 degrees west of south) and XII (bearing of 83 degrees west of north), although indicated on large-scale maps of this century, are lost. The locality of Stone XIV (early May and early August sunsets) on the south-east side of Windmill Hill is littered with sarsen chips and bigger fragments, proving that the stone was broken up on the spot. About half-a-ton of sarsen fragments remains heaped at the side of Horslip Lane like a short low wall (SU 0866 7075).

Outer Stone VIII, originally at SU 0806 6787 on the downs, is probably one of two lichen-covered megaliths now reclining less than a kilometre away at the entrance to

This photograph of a heap of stones is published as a memorial to the loss of a major megalith, Outer Stone XIV. Along Horslip Lane on Windmill Hill once stood the megalith that served as the outer marker stone with regard to the alignment involving the Obelisk and Stone 125 for the early-August and early-May sunsets. Half-a-ton of grey and reddish-brown fragments mark the site of the sarsen that was never in anyone's way.

Firs Farm, Beckhampton (SU 0731 6803). Both are deeply-grooved 'female'-type sarsens of the kind often found in Neolithic monuments. The farmer explained that his men remove megaliths which they consider are in the way. There is no sign of stone-smashing at the VIII site; the megalith seems to have been removed whole. The site's bearing conforms to the Obelisk shadow falling upon Stone 120 at midwinter sunset which is 48 degrees west of south for this hill location.

Outer Stone IX, if it existed, corresponds to the setting of the sun at Hallowe'en (and early February) when the shadow of the Obelisk would engulf Stone 121 of the South Circle. Its bearing would be the opposite of the May sunrise. No stone survives with this bearing (62 degrees west of south) but the 1883 Ordnance Survey maps indicate a group of stones at SU 0755 6835 where the Devizes-Avebury A361 road crosses the ancient Roman road. It is likely they disappeared following road improvements.

Outer Stone XV might be expected in a hill-crest position towards the summit of

Windmill Hill, in a midsummer-sunset alignment with the Obelisk and Stone 126, and nearly in line with Stone 112, Outer-Stone IV and the midwinter sunrise. Nothing can be seen today, but excavation might expose a stone-hole near the westernmost bowl barrow in whose ditch sarsen fragments lie. Lower down the side of Windmill Hill, towards Avebury, the 1883 map indicates a major stone at SU 0905 7099 which could be a placed stone for midsummer-sunset activities at Avebury, although a compass check suggests it may have related to the northern part of Avebury (from which the stone is at 50 degrees west of north—see chapter 8), rather than the southern part (about 48 degrees west of north relative to the Obelisk). Sarsen chips still lie scattered in the plough soil, suggesting that the stone was shattered on the spot.

Predictions as to the whereabouts of *Outer Stones XI* and *XIII*, which I achieved by extending lines from the Obelisk through South Circle Stones 108 and 110 and then westwards, led to the discovery of suitable stones on 5 October, 1998. These megaliths each weigh just over a ton and remain not far from where they had been positioned over 4,000 years ago.

Outer Stone XI, at 81 degrees west of south from the Obelisk, approximates to Stone 108 of the South Circle. It is a flat-bottomed brown sarsen on its back in a hedge on an ancient field boundary (SU 0891 6967). The representation of a left-profile head suggests that it was intended to be a female stone. Much the same can be said of Outer Stone XIII which lies near a field edge at 72 degrees west of north in alignment with South Circle Stone 110 and the Obelisk. The stone may have been spared the fate of many other prehistoric stones because it has been re-used to cover part of a drainage channel into an adjoining ditch (SU 0927 7022). Vague traces of a left-profile head suggest that this might have been viewed as a female stone.

The only outer stone for which I have so far found no trace is Stone III. Autumn field-walking between harvest-time and seed-planting time may eventually yield clues, but in 1998 the relevant fields were under grass. This stone would be expected to correspond with South Circle Stone 122 and the Obelisk on an approximate compass bearing of 76 degrees east of north.

This leaves only Outer Stones I, II, VI and VII.

Outer Stone I. The site of this midsummer sunrise stone, presumably in view of Avebury and on the edge of Totterdown (from which hundreds or thousands of recumbent sarsens were removed by commercial stone-breakers in the nineteenth century) may remain untraceable unless an old written record or map indicating its presence turns up. Its expected 51–52-degree alignment begins with female Stone 105 and the male Obelisk at the midsummer sunrise. Ordnance Survey maps place a lone megalith (Stone Ia) on a 52-degree bearing at a major field corner on Totterdown at SU 1310 7218, but just out of sight of Avebury. It is currently smothered by a dump of field-clearance sarsens. The nearest stone on the Ridgeway to this line is a small grey standing sarsen concealed beneath a thick blackthorn bush which is otherwise in sight of Avebury, but the bearing from the Obelisk is nearer 50 degrees. However, this stone's alternative bearing of 52 degrees when taken from the Cove could be significant in relation to the Cove (see chapter 8).

Outer Stone II. This is the triangular-topped rhomboid sarsen (SU 1242 7032) with inscribed vulva which correlates with the May Festival sunrise (and early August sunrise) when the Obelisk's shadow meets female Stone 106. According to Ordnance Survey maps there is another stone (IIa) on this alignment, at SU 1172 7060 halfway up Green Street hill from Avebury, but it has been taken away in recent years. Where is it now?

Outer Stone VI. This is another female sarsen by the side of the Ridgeway in sight of Avebury. It corresponds with the Obelisk's shadow falling upon Stone 111 at both the early February and the Hallowe'en sunrises. The former occasion was known in Celtic times as Imbolc, the season when the ewes come into milk. *This is a female triangular-topped stone with a seemingly-natural broad groove a metre (3 feet) long and 20 cm (8 ins) wide in its middle.* The stone is 1.5–1.75 metres (5–5¾ feet) in length, a metre (3 feet) wide and 0.6 metre (2 feet) thick. A whitish stone, it weighs about 2½ tons, and when found on 4 May, 1998 it lay fallen with two brown sarsens partly on top of it (at SU 1193 6899). Some or all of the stones had been dragged to the side of the Ridgeway from a nearby position in the field (as suggested by early-twentieth century maps). At the same time the orientation towards the Obelisk at Avebury Henge is the May-Festival bearing again (from here, 62 degrees west of north), but this time for sunset on the eve of the May Festival. The megalith-movers had found a stone with a natural vulva or yoni and set it as a May Eve marker for people near or on the Ridgeway. Erect, it awaited that May Eve sunset (and the early August sunset) when the Obelisk's shadow, at Avebury below, meets Stone 125; it also doubles as an early-February sunrise indicator when the shadow meets Stone III. I returned to the site on 10 September, 1998 to find that female Stone VI had been taken away whole, and the two stones which had lain upon it had been moved about five metres (16 feet) to the south. From the evidence of the disturbance to the turf, the theft had happened only a few days previously. The age of megalith removal is not over, even in a protected World Heritage Park!

Outer Stone VII. At the midwinter sunrise the shadow of the Obelisk meets Stone 112. A mile away, on a similar alignment, is a hill-located megalith, now lost, which Dr Stukeley drew on 15 May, 1724 at the time of sketching the well-preserved disc barrow (SU 1158 6891). Stukeley's standing stone, which appears to have been two or three metres (six to ten feet) high, is on the west-facing side of Overton Hill, over-

The triangular-topped whitish sarsen in the centre of this picture may have been Outer Stone VI. The broad vulva-type groove running down the middle is partly filled with soil and grass. The length of the stone is 1.5 to 1.75 metres (5 to 5¾ feet) and the weight about 2.5 tons. When found in May 1998 it lay flat with the weight of two brown sarsens partly on it. Four months later the brown sarsens had been moved aside and the white sarsen had gone.

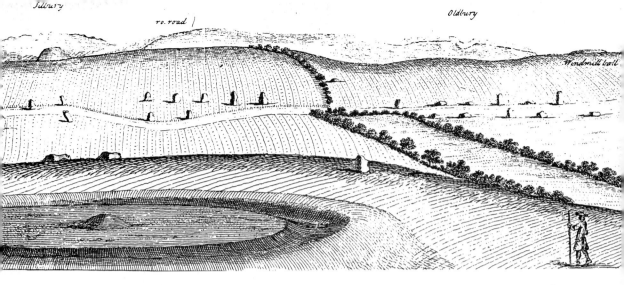

This picture, by William Stukeley, of the Kennet Avenue, shows a megalith standing near the disc barrow on the escarpment north of West Kennet. Whether or not this is Outer Stone VII, it would have been an important stone for it to be raised there. Two others lie nearby. The three stones have long since gone, and the barrow was ploughed out 30 to 40 years ago.

looking Kennet Avenue. Estimation of its co-ordinates (SU 1155 6892) suggests it possibly lay on a midwinter sunrise line (130 degrees east of north) passing through the Obelisk and Stone 126. It may or may not be the sought-after Outer Stone VII. In 1957 Leslie Grinsell reported in the Victoria County History series that the adjacent disc barrow was in good condition, but in 1974 inspectors found that the badly protected monument had been ploughed away. In Stukeley's drawing Silbury is seen peeking over Waden Hill in line between a fallen pair of megaliths just west of the barrow.

Another interesting sarsen is a leaning stone whose bearing from the Obelisk also approximates to the midwinter sunrise line from Avebury (which is, however, just out of sight). It is an impressive four-ton stone in the shape of a female lozenge, whose myriads of embedded quartz fragments scintillate in the sunshine. Two metres (six-and-a-half feet) long, 1.75 metres (5¾ feet) wide and half-a-metre (18 ins) thick, it is by the Ridgeway at SU 1190 6862. This magnificent megalith is 'worthy of Avebury', as John Aubrey might have said. It may or may not be in its original position, for it could have been dragged to the field corner some time this century from a position 80 metres (87 yards) east into the field. The 1883 map shows five sarsens within 80–200 metres (87–220 yards) whose positions inside the field could still be identified today by archaeological techniques. Falkner's Circle in the valley bottom lies close to or on the line between the South Circle, Stukeley's Stone and this lozenge stone.

The surviving stones discussed here, even the remnants of number XIV, deserve scheduling as Ancient Monuments. As part of the archaeology and sacred landscape of Avebury, the undamaged stones should be re-erected, for standing stones are safer from damage and theft than fallen stones hidden in the grass. None of the lesser known

This drawing by William Stukeley usefully depicts Stones 125 and 126 of the South Circle and the Ring Stone. In the foreground, left to right, are Stones 107, 106 and 105 of the South Circle followed by Stones 103 and 101 and in the far distance, centre left, Stones 126 and 125. Nearer is the unnamed stone which may be Z-stone ix, and to the left is the Obelisk viewed end-on. The Ring Stone, prominent by its dark hole, is in the gap between 101 and 103. At the back from left to right are Stones 97, 98 and 1. Lastly, in the distance at the right edge of the picture is Avenue Stone 4a.

sites can be regarded as safe yet, as witness the disappearance of Outer Stone VI in early September 1998. Those stones which have gone missing in the last 60 years (since the last commercial sarsen-breakers closed down) have been removed whole. Where have they gone? Lastly, remember that along some of the sight-lines more than one stone may have been set up to align with the sarsens of the South Circle—so the positions of more Outer Stones may still be discovered. In particular, where such stones were located quite near to Avebury (e.g. IV, V and XIII), more distant ones on hills probably existed too, of which clues or traces have yet to be found.

Besides the five surviving South Circle Stones which appear to show feminine characteristics (101–103, 105, 106), all the missing Stones 111–112, 120–121 and 125–126 could function as feminine stones in the enactment of a Sacred Marriage at the solstices and at the May, August, November and February festivals, if these were celebrated. Missing Stone 123 also occupies an equinoctial position at the east, while the symmetrically-placed Stones 122 and 124 correspond to intermediate solar settings. The directions of the remaining destroyed Stones 107 to 110 at the west can be evaluated to provide calendar dates as well. In this way a sun-based calendar can be developed to account for 15 of the 29 megaliths of the South Circle in which each stone experiences a watchable 'marriage'. This suggests that the Obelisk may have functioned as the Sky Father's representative or member on earth, as I proposed in *Stonehenge: the Secret of the Solstice* for the Heel Stone at Stonehenge.

I have found no definite indications at the South Circle to suggest an interest in the moon, so it appears more and more likely that these stones were planned at a time in the third millennium when it was the sun which monopolised—if not literally over-shadowed—the people's attention. Lunar concerns may belong to an earlier age, for instance as appears possible for the earliest phase of Stonehenge, about 2950 BCE.

To sum up what we know about the perimeter stones of the South Circle, it can be argued that the entire ring of stones was intended to be female. This could mean that the stone circle was a female-genital shrine of fertility or Earth Goddess temple, with a male stone erect in the middle.

If this conclusion is right, it is possible that Avebury may have been spiritually not unlike later examples which are better known. For instance, as summarised by Barbara Walker (1983), the Irish sacred grove at Tara was the local Earth Mother's shrine, with a central stone pillar which represented the God Fal (hence, phallus). In India and Tibet the ubiquitous Goddess Tara lives on in holy worship, and at one time was revered in probably all Aryan-populated and pre-Indo-European lands. The name Tara comes from the same root as the *Taramata* (Earth Mother), Latin *Terra Mater*, Hebrew *Terah* and Gaulish *Taranis*, and was in use in Celtic Britain as it was in Ireland and Wales. In addition, the Sky Father's name, meaning thunder, was *Taran* in Wales and *Torann* in Ireland. In remotest times the fanfare Taran-tara began as a magic call expressing the union of the two deities.

This is as far as analysis of the megaliths of Avebury's South Circle goes at present. We can imagine that on the eve of the May Festival the sun goes to bed in a shadowed union with the Earth Mother as represented by Stone 125, and rises in the morning still united with her in the likeness of the great female Stone 106. In this context it is known from recorded English traditions that the May Day festival began the preceding evening with joyful merrymaking between couples in the woods. Six weeks later, at the solstice, one may speculate that the sun goes to bed on Midsummer's Eve with Stone 126 and rises in the morning still joined but with the union transferred to female Stone 105.

5

THE STONES COME TO LIFE

Stones of the Z-feature and south-east quadrant of the Great Circle

In the mid-1660s John Aubrey wrote of Avebury in his *Monumenta Britannica*: 'Round about the Graffe [i.e. dyke or ditch] on the edge or border of it are pitched on end huge stones, as big, or rather bigger than those at Stoneheng: but rude, and unhewn as they are drawn out of the earth: whereas those of Stoneheng are roughly hewn.'

At first sight the stones do appear rude, yet their very roughness masks a mystifying form of art. As I proposed in chapter 1, *every surviving, undamaged standing stone, if not already sexually symbolic because of its outline or through possession of some explicit natural feature, has a head upon it, usually in profile, most often human, and always with an eye. Such is the nature of the images and the distinctiveness of the symbolism that the majority may be regarded as 'feminine' rather than 'masculine', as I hope to make clear.*

Some 4,500 years ago the unhewn stones were set on end in circles and avenues, but afterwards, as the centuries passed, a secret art form was practised upon them; and this was done in such a way that most of the profiles would be known to no one but leaders and their confidants, priests, initiates and the devout. Unfortunately hundreds of the stones have been destroyed but the remaining ones and their sculptures, having survived the weather and vandalistic attacks, must be properly protected for future generations because some of the exquisite carvings are not easy to detect, having features that are quite faintly outlined and vulnerable to the feet of unknowing climbers.

In some cases the Avebury people may have done no work at all on a stone, choosing it because a profile was already apparent. In others a suggestion of a profile may have been noted, and a certain amount of pecking or carving was done in order to enhance it. Sometimes it was an eye that was added, or a mouth or nose; or some modification was made to a facial profile. And in most cases it was a left-facing profile that resulted.

* * *

All five surviving stones of the South Circle group were classified by Isobel Smith as female, or Type B, on the basis of Keiller's definition of stone types, and we have seen that *Stones 105 and 106* are irrefutably female by virtue of being vulvar stones. *Stone 101* is female too with its left-profile head facing inwards to the Obelisk when viewed from the west, especially between 4 and 5.30 p.m. in the summer.

Stone 103, like *Stone 102*, possesses considerable 'angularity', a feminine attribute included in Keiller's broad definition of Type B stones. To make it clearer, *we can say that lozenge stones are first and foremost Type B or obviously female stones, while imperfect lozenges and irregular triangles or triangular-topped stones are also essentially female Type B. The same applies to megaliths with natural major clefts, near-vertical fissures, holes, cup-marks and multi-pitted surfaces.* Stones 102 and 103 are examples of female angular stones that have pronounced clefts. Stone 103 has a left-profile head visible at midday facing north. On its western side there is a full face which acquires well-formed lips in the later afternoon (4 to 5 p.m. BST). These are best seen in the summer months. The mark on the forehead, which it owes to a widening fracture of the rock, is reminiscent of the jewelled pendants worn in this position by Hindu girls.

All six standing stones of *the Z-feature*, numbered iii to viii, display heads in female left-profile. They are the smallest sarsens at Avebury, each lighter than half-a-ton. Keiller's team discovered them buried in pits, and supposed that they had been concealed in the mediaeval period because the burial of one of the Great Circle stones (Stone 9) can be dated to this time. However, as Peter Ucko and his colleagues pointed out, villagers had told Stukeley about stone-burial activities taking place in the century prior to his, so the period of stone burial lasted longer than previously thought and we cannot be sure when the Z-stones were buried.

This face on Stone 103 (centre right) of the South Circle is best viewed in the summer sunshine of late afternoon. When part of the bulky rock alongside develops into a left-profile head, the overall impression is that of mother and daughter, or age and youth. Photographs taken at 5.30 p.m. BST, 4.30 GMT, on 29 May.

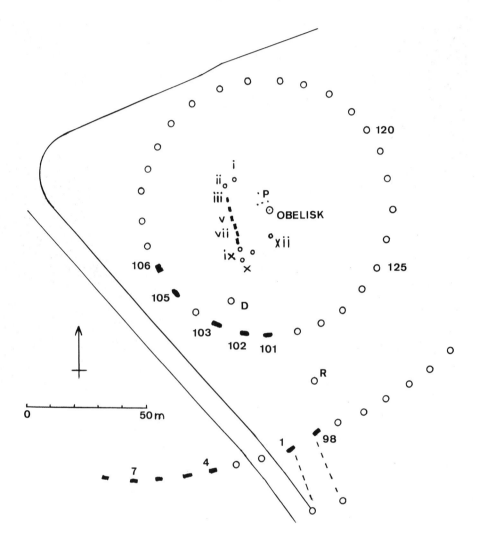

The South Circle, the Z-stones, and part of the South-East Quadrant of the Great Circle. Stones present are shown black; stones absent are indicated by open circles. P indicates the four earth-filled pits, and R the Ring Stone. The entrance stones from the Kennet Avenue are Stones 98 and 1. Stone 106 is the principal female stone. The calendrical stones are Stones 105–112 and 120–126.

The most northerly of the surviving Z-stones is *Stone iii* which has a north-facing left-profile head, best seen between 5 and 6 p.m. in the sunshine of the summer months. On its western side is a natural hole at the centre of a broad nearly-circular dished area 180mm (7 ins) in diameter, which the sun reaches at around midday.

All six surviving Z-stones have left-facing heads. The four shown here are Stones iii and iv (top) and vii and viii (bottom). Photographs were taken as follows: Stone iii, 4.30 p.m. GMT (29 May), Stone iv, 2.30 p.m. GMT (18 November); Stone vii, 10.00 a.m. GMT (30 April); Stone viii, 4.30 p.m. GMT (29 May).

(Left) Stone v at the Z-setting within the South Circle. Possible snake- or crone-goddess head photographed at 11.00 a.m. BST, 10.00 GMT, on 12 May.

(Right) Besides the left-facing head on Z-stone vi there is a second head turned the opposite way, but it is only for a few minutes at around 10.30 a.m. GMT, 11,30 BST, that the second, male head has an eye 'with which to see'. The stone possibly played a role in some now forgotten mythological tale. This short-lived male head is set to face the head of the Snake Goddess or Crone Goddess on Z-stone v.

Stone iv displays its left-profile head well in the winter between 2 and 3 p.m.

Stone v is interesting because it has a left-profile serpent-like head which shows up well, facing south, only when the eye (probably carved) is set off by shadow between the hours of 10 and 11 a.m. GMT, or 11 and 12 BST. This is one of three similar snake-heads or 'Crone Goddess' heads that I have found at Avebury Henge (the other two are on stones of the Great Circle, see chapters 7 and 8).

On *Stone vi* at about 10.30 a.m. GMT, 11.30 BST, the left eye of one head and the right eye of a second head are set off by shadow simultaneously, as though they could be non-identical twins in some mythical story. Another possible left-profile head faces westwards, its left eye at its best in sunshine between 1 and 3 p.m. in the summer.

The left-profile head on *Stone vii* is turned to the west. The sun needs to be out at about 11 a.m. in the summer or 10 in the winter for it to be seen. Finally, *Stone viii* has a north-facing left-profile beaked head with a small eye visible in the sunshine at 5.30 p.m. summertime.

Blocks of Lower Chalk were found in some of the stone-holes of the Z-feature, implying that these stones were erected at around the time when the *bottom* of the great dyke was being dug out. The Z-feature is therefore a late addition to the mega-lithic complex.

Most or all of Stones i, ii, ix, x and xi had been buried too, but were afterwards discovered and destroyed by villagers, though when is not known. According to Keiller a twelfth stone, xii, disappeared without passing through a burial phase. On the other hand, it seems that Stone ix can be matched to the unattributed standing stone sketched and mapped by William Stukeley before it was destroyed.

In searching for the stone-hole of this missing sarsen Keiller's team found a vacant hole a little to the north of Stone 103, which they attributed to an unidentified mega-lith, Stone D. By its side was a stake-hole which contained weathered sherds of Bell Beaker pottery. This indicates a late date for the erection of the stone which may relate in some way to Silbury Hill whose flat summit is just visible from this part of Avebury. Practically in a line are Silbury, Stone 4 (of the Great Circle), Stone D and Z-Stone x.

Stukeley's unidentified stone appears on two maps, according to which it was placed either 55 or 60 feet (18 metres) from the Obelisk and 110 feet (34 metres) from Stone 101, the distance between Stone 101 and the Obelisk being given as 160 feet (49 metres). This means that it cannot be Stone D, contrary to Isobel Smith's suggestion, but is most likely Stone ix from the Z-setting. Peter Ucko and his colleagues (1991) proposed that it was either Stone ix, x or xi. Stukeley's drawing makes the stone female Type B, and not dissimilar from the biggest of the surviving Z-stones.

Another female stone is the one which William Stukeley called the Ring Stone, but it was 'taken away' two centuries ago.

He describes it as 'an odd stone standing, not of great bulk. It has a hole wrought in it . . .' The word 'odd' refers to its position, neither part of a circle nor in a line of stones. Its height appears to be half that of the nearest megaliths, and its hole is a total perforation offset from the middle and possibly as much as 25cm (10ins) in diameter. When the stone-hole of the absent Ring Stone was examined in 1939, the broken stump of the stone was exposed, and this was then re-erected above ground. Lumps of Lower Chalk from the base of the dyke had been used as packing.

Perforated standing stones were common in ancient Britain and Brittany. Traditions associated with holed stones which survived into historic times hint at fertility-related usages, like hand-fasting at marriage ceremonies, appeals to end sterility, and prayers for healing and health-giving.

Close to the Z-stones and the Obelisk are four flat concrete discs. They mark the sites of prehistoric pits whose contents were found to be fine, chalk-free, dark-brown soil which had been carried there from some distance. The purpose of this high-quality fertile soil is not known, but a ritual use is not unlikely. Michael Dames (1977) quoted a wedding practice from central Africa in which rich alluvial soil is rubbed into new-lyweds after the bridal night as a last propitious act of the ceremony, and suggested that the British fondness for the wedding-cake tradition has similar significance. Near the concrete discs are seven post-holes which Isobel Smith believes held maypoles because May Day dancing was still being performed there as late as the nineteenth and twentieth centuries.

Moving on to the megaliths of the Great Circle, whose number has been estimated as 98, we find that only two great stones of this part of the south-east sector are upright today. Numbered 1 and 98, these immense stones stand over four metres (thirteen feet) high and were placed nearly eight metres (twenty-six feet) apart on either side of the chalk causeway at the southern entrance to the monument. The modern road passes to the west of the prehistoric entry point and covers the hole in which Stone 2 used to stand. *Stone 97*, a huge Type B megalith to the east, was sketched by William Stukeley, but nothing can be learnt from his drawings as regards carved heads. It is an angular, quasi-lozenge megalith.

The angular *Stone 98*, whose mass is about 45 tons, has three left-profile heads on it. Most impressive is the head of a dignified personage carved into the eastern edge of the inner face of the rock. If the figure is female, as its left-sidedness suggests, it is interesting that femininity was assigned to what appears to be a solemn priest-like head. Does the carving represent a priestess or some other female in authority, or is it a woman with a high headdress reminiscent of Breton peasants in traditional dress on a feast day? This excellent 'portrait' sculpture stands out late in the day in the summer sunshine.

Stone 98's second head is on the west-facing edge. Seen from below when the sun is shining in the late afternoon on a summer's day, it towers above the observer. The third head, for which the morning sunshine is needed, is on the south side of the mega-lith and faces its companion Stone 1 to the west.

Stone 1, with a mass of about 50 tons, has acquired the name Devil's Chair on account of its south-facing seat which has a wide pipe-hole or chimney open to the sky above. Devi's Chair would be more appropriate (*devi* being an archaic word, still in use, for goddess), because a huge left-facing head appears in the early-morning sun-shine facing west. However, Stone 1, like 98, is both an Entrance Stone and a Guardian Stone, so the Ancient Britons provided it with a great right-profile head as well, to face Stone 98's third left-profile head. The former, visible in the early-afternoon sun-shine, occupies the whole of Stone 1.

Stone 1. This guardian stone at the southern entrance to Avebury has a seat on its south-facing side. In the morning the head looks left (upper photograph taken 9 April at 7.30 a.m. BST, 6.30 GMT). By the afternoon the shadows here produced an enormous head facing right (lower photograph taken on 25 October at 1 p.m. GMT, 2 p.m. BST).

The only other stones in this south-east quadrant are *Stones 77 and 78*, both lying 200 metres (220 yards) away near the eastern entrance. There appears to be a left-facing head on the angular Type B Stone 78 whose mass is about 17 tons. Stone 77, less than two metres (six feet) long, is only a fragment of a bigger stone. According to A. C. Smith (1885) who probed and dug for stones in 1881, fifteen megaliths of the eastern half of the Great Circle are buried along the arc where Stukeley wrote, 'Demolish'd by Tom Robinson, Anno 1700'. Isobel Smith interprets this as specifying ten stones in this south-east sector, most likely *Stones 79–80, 83–88*, and either *Stones 90–91* or *91–92*, while the other five are in the north-east sector (see chapter 8).

* * *

Let's pause for a moment and consider the subtlety and craftsmanship of the numerous carvings belonging to the south-east quadrant. Many of the heads and profiles rely on strong sunshine at the right time of day. Some are affected by the seasons as well. Often a slight hollow, meaningless until then, is transformed by the moving rays of the low or high sun into a skilfully executed eye, mouth or ear—a careful feat of sculpture sometimes achieved by limited pecking with a hard-stone tool.

As far as possible the sculptors took advantage of accidental forms which suggested images in the eye of the beholder. In that sense it may be called opportunistic art. The Avebury people could conjure shapes into heads and figures as well as we can. They would have believed that the images in the stones were as much a divine gift as were the sarsens. Sometimes no further work was needed; on others the widening of a crack or the addition of a line or hollow was enough to animate the stone. Sometimes the result was like a caricature, but often the work led to an acceptable rendering of a human image.

There seems to have been no wish to seek reality in the more fastidious Mediterranean Neolithic tradition. If this had been so, the ingenious handiwork would have been so obvious that it would have been common knowledge long ago. Instead, the aim was to create forms and figures, heads and profiles, which were so slight and usually so dependent on the sun that only those in the know would be aware of their presence. Stonemasons, priests, priestesses and acolytes would do the minimum work necessary; and, in course of time, initiates and believers would learn the secrets, possibly as part of rites and the telling of epic stories and tribal myths.

6

THE SPIRITS IN THE STONES

The stones of the south-west quadrant

Eleven megaliths remain in the south-west quadrant of the Great Circle. Six had been buried in mediaeval times or later (Stones 4–6, 9–10, 16) and so were spared the fate of others in more recent centuries—for example, Stones 3, 11, 13, 15 and 17–18 which had stood for longer but then suffered destruction by fire. The buried stones, some damaged, were dug up by Keiller's team in 1938 and re-erected, as were Stones 7 and 12 which had been only partially buried and the fallen Stone 14. Stones 19–23 had also been buried but later rediscovered and burnt. Part of Stone 24 had been incorporated into the building of the village forge. Only one stone had escaped the wrath of centuries and was still upright, and that was Stone 8.

Again, many megaliths in this section have heads, and there are dozens more throughout the rest of Avebury and along the Kennet Avenue. Can we read any more into these than we have already? The answer may lie in folklore, for throughout what is left of the megalithic world in the rest of Britain, traditional knowledge and belief may possibly provide a clue.

In 1937 Leslie Grinsell, writing in the journal *Folklore*, cited traditions from western Britain and elsewhere in which megaliths were held to be maidens or wedding guests

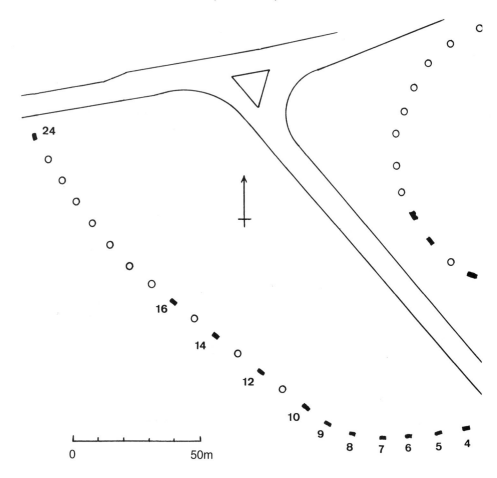

The south-west quadrant of the Great Circle. Stone 9 is the Barber Stone.

transformed into stone, or were said to dance or speak or to go to a stream to drink or bathe at night.

From this standpoint Grinsell stressed the countrywide prevalence of the common theme that life appears to be 'so intimately connected with prehistoric stones it may well be a garbled form of early belief.' In other words, it suggests 'the idea of primitive man investing them with properties of living beings'. Is this how the stones of Avebury were regarded in the Megalithic Age? Were carved stones treated as living things harbouring spirits, while sarsens displaying sex-related symbols (vulvas, holes, fissures, breasts, triangles, lozenges, phalluses) stored the essence of fertility deities?

* * *

The megalith nearest the main road is *Stone 4*. A left-profile head facing west can be viewed from the south in the late-afternoon summer sunshine. The stone's southern side is strangely dotted with hundreds of tiny rings and U-shapes, looking as if they were impressed into the surface. Whatever the likely natural origin of these marks, they may have been enough to give the stone some mystical quality. A hole towards the centre-base of the stone could have been respected as a yoni symbol in megalithic times.

Stone 5, a multi-fissured megalith, has a left-profile head facing west which requires good mid-afternoon sunshine to set it off. A simple right-profile head, which can be seen in mid-morning sunshine looking towards the distant Obelisk, might be a feature known in Neolithic times, but this is unclear. The head at the eastern edge of *Stone 6*, an angular Type B female stone, appears in oblique frontal view with both eyes showing. To see it, crouch down and look upwards, preferably with the sun out at 8 or 9 in the morning. An indistinct left-profile head, visible on its northern side facing east in the early-morning sun, has not been included in this survey.

Stone 7, another angular Type B stone, is seen at its best early in the morning and late in the evening. The northern side acquires a possible left-profile head with eye and mouth on midsummer evening after 8.30 p.m. BST, not long before sunset. On its north-eastern edge, positioned facing north, the right side of a refined head can be seen for a while around 8.30 GMT, 9.30 BST.

I have not included what could be a left-profile head on the south-west edge of *Stone 8*, which appears in bright sunshine. This is a Type B stone which is really a lozenge resting on one of its sides instead of balancing on a point. On its south side there is an improbable vulvar hole, with a vertical groove slightly above it. Higher still there is an upward-pointing arrow which could be a surveyor's benchmark.

Stone 9 is the 'Barber's Stone', which fell in the fourteenth century, killing a man who was preparing the pit into which the stone was to be toppled. The man had been carrying a pair of hinged iron scissors and a small iron implement which may have been a lancet or probe. He may have been a barber-surgeon or possibly a tailor or cobbler. With him were two silver pennies of Edward I, minted in Canterbury not later than 1307, and a silver sterling from Toul in Lorraine which cannot have come into circulation in England before c.1310–15. The expert opinion of J. D. A. Thompson is that the coins set the date of the owner's death between 1320 and 1325 (Smith, 1965: 177–9). Keiller made this find in 1938, and presented the skeleton to the Royal College of Surgeons in London, but the bombing raids of 1941 destroyed the barber's last remains for ever.

The finding of the skeleton proved the truth of a folk rumour which had persisted in the village for hundreds of years—that a falling stone had killed a man in the remote past. A different version of the story was published by O. Meyrick in the *Wiltshire*

The southern side of Stone 4 is covered with hundreds of tiny circles and U-shapes—naturally created—which may have added to the appeal of the stone in the eyes of the Avebury people. Its yoni symbolism is further supplemented by the central hole towards its base. A remarkable small head appears on this stone, facing left, for a short spell in the late afternoon. This photograph was taken at 4.30 p.m. BST, 3.30 GMT, on 25 August.

Two views of Stone 5 suggest left-facing heads. The left-hand picture was taken at 8.00 a.m. BST, 7.00 GMT, on 14 April; the right-hand picture was taken at 2.30 p.m. BST, 1.30 GMT, on 29 April.

Archaeological Magazine in 1959. It arose from a letter written by one John Saunders, who spent more than a week in Avebury in August 1712. Here he heard the legend of a cobbler who had been mending shoes on the Sabbath under one of the great stones. When he got up the stone fell, but as he escaped unhurt, this was interpreted as divine intervention intended to discourage him from ever again working on a Sunday.

The stone is of the female-lozenge type, balanced on a point. An unclear left-sided head appears at the top when viewed from the west in sunshine.

The female left-profile head on *Stone 10*, which is turned south-westwards, can be seen at any time when looking edge-on from the south-east. The head and neck occupy the entire stone. Particularly good in early-morning sunshine, it is the best surviving head in this quadrant and has a very dignified air about it. At the north-east at the top it is possible to make out what could be a right-sided head with headgear or 'crown'. It needs sunshine and shadow before 10 a.m. BST, 9 a.m. GMT, to see this and the entire effect may be accidental—but it could have been known to the ancient Britons.

The east side of Stone 5 has an unusual head, here illuminated by early-morning sunshine: 8.00 a.m. BST, 7.00 GMT, on 14 April.

The Barber's Stone in the south-west quadrant. Stone 9 is the angular type B stone which killed a man while he was attempting to undermine and fell it in the fourteenth century. Photographed at 8.30 a.m. GMT, 25 October.

Another huge lozenge balanced on a point. This is Stone 12, in the south-west quadrant. Some of the lozenge stones appear not to have heads or faces on them. Photographed at 8.00 a.m. BST, 7.00 GMT, 14 April.

Stone 12 is another Type B stone selected for its lozenge shape and balanced on a point. This establishes its femininity, but it may also have an imperfect left-profile head at its north-western edge on the south-west side of the stone (seen in summer evening sunshine but not included in the survey.).

From the north-west *Stone 14* has an animal-like air to it—a frog or seal perhaps—with a left eye which becomes prominent for a while after midday. Its overall shape identifies it as female. A probable left-profile head on its western side can be seen in the late afternoon, and there may be a left-profile head at its south-eastern edge when seen from the east in the early morning (8 a.m.) and a left-profile head viewed from the north on a summer evening. More photographs in sunshine are needed of this stone, and also of Type B *Stone 16* which has a reasonable left-sided head at its south-eastern edge facing east. It is visible at any time but is improved by sunshine in the early morning.

Lastly, the partly destroyed *Stone 24* has a fair left-profile head on its less damaged south-east surface, but it is unclear whether this feature was known in the Neolithic age. Alexander Keiller rescued this angular stone from the foundations of the nearby premises of the village blacksmith (Fowler's Forge) when it was demolished. An iron wedge, used for breaking the megalith into smaller pieces, remains embedded near the base on its northern side.

This much damaged stone was found upon dismantling Fowler's Forge in the 1930s. On the less-damaged south-eastern side there is a good mouth and the chance that a left eye, natural or otherwise, previously existed as well. Photographed at 11.45 am BST, 10.45 GMT, 13 May.

7

SYMBOLS OF THE FEMININE
The great stones of the north-west quadrant

When Alexander Keiller began work at the Avebury Circles in 1937, only four stones (32, 33, 44, 46) stood upright in this north-western sector, while a further six, five of them broken, could be seen inside a boundary wall (Stones 34–36, 40–42). Stones 30 and 31 were found below ground. The remaining five (37–39, 43, 45) had been shattered by fire two or three centuries earlier and wholly lost. When Keiller's restoration work was finished, 12 stones stood in their original sockets, the ones we are so happy to see today.

Stone 30, which is slightly damaged, has what looks like a left-side head facing south on its eastern side. The area around a natural hole forming the eye appears to have been widened by pecking and, being slightly shallower, lichen has taken hold. The stone is female Type B on Keiller's definition.

A likely head facing left appears in good sunlight on the western side of *Stone 31* in the early afternoon. This damaged Type B stone may also have a heavily damaged downward-pointing triangle in the middle of its eastern side. Whether natural or not, such a female feature could explain the choice of this Type B megalith, especially because at the apex of the triangle there is a suggestive deep round hole. The stone was buried by the villagers hundreds of years ago, and any defacement of the possible

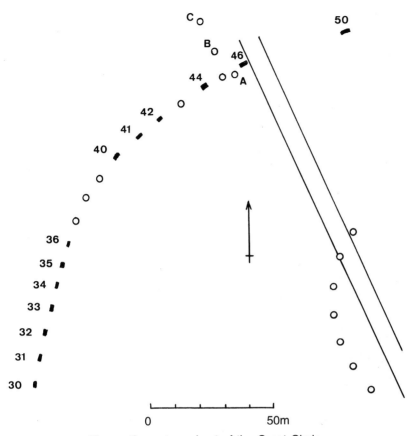

The north-west quadrant of the Great Circle.

symbol may have been done then. The feature is best seen in the summer at 9–10 a.m. BST. Some people may doubt its validity but as the next megalith, Stone 32, displays a Goddess-type symbol in the middle of its eastern face, we need to consider the probability that the Avebury people were aware of these features and their meanings, and chose to place these stones side by side.

Stone 32 is above all remarkable for its resplendent forward-facing female torso, illustrated on p. 8. The deep yoni or vulva and slight suggestion of breasts show up well in the slanting late-evening sunshine of high summer. A good time is 7.30 to 8 p.m. BST in June, and this month of course includes the summer solstice sunset. Situated at ground level, the vulva is also illuminated obliquely at the solstice from about 5 a.m. BST for an hour or two. Although the hole is a natural property of the stone, the 12-ton megalith was clearly selected because of it and angled so that light from the summer sunrise could reach it. By representing the female form Stone 32

In the middle of the eastern side of Stone 31—a Type B female megalith—is what appears
to be a damaged inverted triangle with a hole at its apex. Stones 32 and 34 also have
enigmatic symbols or images at the centres of their eastern sides. Photographed at
10.15 a.m. BST, 9.15 GMT, 17 October.

could have been viewed as a Goddess Stone and held to possess female fertilising
powers.

Another hint about the presence of a female deity at this stone comes from the shape
of a hollow area in the middle of the east-facing side, where a sunken outline resembles the familiar shoulder-and-body images of Neolithic Breton goddesses. The outline is also similar to the so-called 'Goddess image' on trilithon stone 57 at Stonehenge.
This weather-worn feature was originally created by tree-root action in geological
times. Either it is entirely natural or it has been 'improved' a little by the art of the
mason (see picture p. 65). Certainly, the people who raised the megaliths chose to set
side by side two stones whose eastern faces both have central symbols which can be
interpreted as typical of an age of Goddess belief.

Stone 33 is a huge megalith, wider than it is high—another Keiller Type B stone likely to be feminine. It has a left-profile head on its western side turned to the north, visible when illuminated towards sunset in the summer.

Stone 34 is a lozenge type of female stone, slightly damaged and with no obvious head. In the middle of its eastern inner side is a heart-shaped motif which is probably not man-made but, like the east-facing images on Stones 31 and 32, may have been given a symbolic significance in the spirit of the times. The outline of a faint downward-pointing triangle can be made out when the sun shines on it in the early afternoon.

The next megalith, *Stone 35*, is another likely Goddess Stone. From whatever direction it is viewed, it has an unmistakable sphinx-like quality, with an enigmatic head on a strong, thick neck facing west (perhaps seen at its best when its north-eastern side is sunlit after sunrise in June). At first sight the great head seems to be masked or defaced—a puzzle that is not resolved until the morning sun illuminates the stone at the best angle. Then a different head appears—on its eastern side, where there is a female left-sided face looking south. This may represent the forbidding but serene Crone Goddess or Snake Goddess, visible from sunrise onwards at all dates of the year. However, the best time to take photographs is when the sun is shining on it at a grazing angle, between 11 and 12 BST, or 10 and 11 GMT. This image resembles the one on Z-Stone v close to the Obelisk (see chapter 5) and Stone 68 will provide a third.

When I examined this stone again I found what seemed to be two more left-sided faces or heads. To find number two you should stoop a little and look upwards from the east at mid-morning. Number three shows up best in complete profile in the afternoon. Together the three left-sided heads make up a trinity of female faces or Goddesses on the same stone, while the puzzling head—the 'inscrutible sphinx'—could be that of a right-sided male.

Stones 36 and 40 are of the female lozenge-type but damaged. On the narrow south side of Stone 36, the left side of a sheep's head can be seen in good sunshine. The eye appears well between 9 and 10 BST. This stone may also have traces of an east-facing left-profile head on its undamaged northern edge, visible at mid-morning, but this could be accidental. *Stone 41* is represented only by a small standing fragment, and *Stone 42*, although partly restored, is so badly damaged that we cannot be certain about its outline or any head carvings.

It is another matter with Type B *Stone 44* which has remained in position as an upright stone since prehistoric times. Four of the heads include three lightly worked left-sided profiles and a peculiar left-sided 'pop-eyed' head of what may be a mythical beast. There seems to be a fifth head, right-sided this time, on the east side looking towards the northern entrance of the henge, as a guardian might do on a Guardian Stone.

Finally, standing as a lozenge-shaped sentinel next to the main road is another female fertility stone, *Stone 46*. It is known as the Swindon Stone or Diamond Stone. Apart

The lozenge-type Stone 34 has an enigmatic symbol in the middle of its eastern face, here obliquely illuminated by the rays of the midsummer rising sun. Although natural in origin, the worshippers probably had some supernatural explanation for the heart-shaped symbol. Photographed at 5.42 a.m. BST, 4.42 GMT, 21 June.

Stone 35. In the early morning sunshine of high summer the stone assumes a sphinx-like air with its possible right-facing head. Photograph taken at 5.45 a.m. BST, 4.45 GMT, 21 June. The other three heads found on this stone form a trinity in left-facing profile, one resembling the Snake Goddess or Crone Goddess.

(Above) Left-profile head on Stone 35, possibly representing the Snake Goddess or Crone Goddess, illuminated by the morning sunshine. Photograph taken at 11.45 a.m. BST, 10.45 GMT, on 9 September.

(Right) Another of the heads in left profile on Stone 35. Photographed at 2.15 p.m. GMT on 23 October. This is effectively the left-side equivalent of the right-side head shown in the first photograph.

The head of a sheep on the southern edge of lozenge Stone 36. Photographed at 10.00 a.m. BST, 9.00 GMT on 25 October.

The Diamond Stone, number 46, stands at the northern entrance to the henge.
It was a guardian stone like Stones 1 and 98 at the south, but unlike them there is no
more than the smallest hint of heads on it—yet that may have been enough for the ancient
Britons. The stone's grandeur emanates from the power that the people put into it when
they balanced a 60-ton lozenge on a point.

from a possible Rorschach left-facing head at its top north-west edge at 6 p.m. BST
and another right-sided one close to the road on its south side, I have not found any
definite heads on this 60-ton megalith, but its inherent feminine symbolism, emanat-
ing powerfully from its diamond or lozenge shape, is acknowledged by cultures everywhere. The word 'dia-mond' is important as an explanation for the basic lozenge shape.
This originates from the word-combination 'dia' (for goddess) and 'mond' (for world).
In other countries lozenge-shaped diamonds were sacred to the Mother Goddess
because they dominated other stones through their extreme hardness. It is possible that
in the age of Goddess worship the local people regarded the supremely hard sarsens
in the same way, and saw lozenge-shaped sarsens as especially potent symbols.

The Wiltshire dialect word for these stones is 'sazzen'—arguably the genuine origin of the word—which has practically the same pronunciation as the 'sassens' of India where the word is in use for similar ancient monoliths traditionally associated in belief and ritual with Mahadevi, the Great (*maha*) Goddess (*devi*). 'Sazzen' is just one of several words in our language known to have close affinities with Sanskrit and pre-Indo-European words. H. C. Bentnall has noted that the Rollright Stones in Oxfordshire are occasionally referred to as 'the Sarsen Stones' although they are oolitic limestone and not sarsen in the geological sense of silica-cemented sandstone. In other words, they are 'sarsen' in the etymological sense of being 'sazzen' like other megaliths from the Neolithic Age.

Stone 32, with female torso and vulva on its northern side, also has this potential goddess symbol on its eastern side. This weather-worn mark is in the category of the shouldered body images typical of numerous carved Breton mother goddesses, and it recalls the much-discussed 'Goddess outline' on trilithon 57 at Stonehenge. Although of natural origin, believers may have thought it was a sign or a 'gift' of the Goddess. Photographed 9.30 am BST, 8.30 GMT, 18 October.

8

MIDSUMMER MARRIAGE

The north-east quadrant, the North Circle, and Cove

Of the 27 Great Circle stones in this quadrant, numbered 47 to 73, only three are in sight. Stones 50 and 68 have never fallen, but the splendid megalith *Stone 73* lies sadly alongside the eastern entrance to the henge. This megalith deserves to be raised again as soon as possible.

In 1881 A. C. Smith probed this part of the circle and thought that at least five more stones lay beneath the turf and could be recovered. On the modern numbering scheme these are believed to be *Stones 69–71* and either *Stones 56–57* or *57–58* (I. Smith, 1965).

At the east side of the northern entrance *Stone 47* used to stand as the companion to Stone 46 whose top is now 4.5 metres (14ft 9ins) above the ground. Stukeley saw and admired it in its fallen state: 'In the north entrance of the town one of the stones, of a most enormous bulk, fell down and broke in the fall . . . It measured full 22 feet long.' Isobel Smith suggests that its above-ground height when standing was about 18 feet, or 5.5 metres.

Stone 50, standing alone at the north, is wider than it is high. A Keiller Type B stone, it has a cleft at its top, reminiscent of Stone 103 in the South Circle. Its southern side may represent the left profile of a sheep's head with upright ears, or perhaps a hare, but you need afternoon sunshine to see this as a possibility.

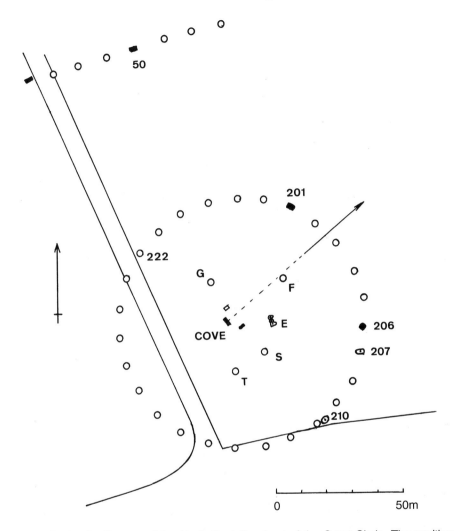

The North Circle, the Cove, and the North-East Quadrant of the Great Circle. The position of Stone F relative to the Cove and Stone 201 is a best approximation using measurements provided by William Stukeley and R. Crocker. Fallen stones 207, 210 and E are marked with a dot in the middle. The direction of Neolithic midsummer sunrise over Hackpen Hill is also shown.

The remaining Great Circle stone visible today is *Stone 68* near Avebury's eastern entrance. It is another Keiller Type B female stone. Low down there is a head best seen, at any time of day, by standing back on the edge of the dyke. It is a south-facing left-profile head, similar to the human/snake type visible on Stones 35 and v of the Z-setting. Like these others, the head may represent the Snake Goddess or Crone Goddess.

Stone 68, north-east sector. This is the third representation of a possible Snake Goddess at Avebury. Whereas it is visible at any time of day, it is best seen when sunlit early in the morning. This photograph was taken at 5.20 a.m. GMT, 6.20 BST, on 21 June.

There may be a second left-profile head on this stone, which appears in the late afternoon sunshine in summer.

The 27-stone North Circle stands in this part of the henge, the counterpart of the 29-stone South Circle discussed in chapters 3 and 4. Four stones of this once important ring remain. Stones 201 and 206 are still upright, while *Stones 207 and 210* await

(Left) This east-facing head on Stone 206 can be viewed from both right and left sides. The right-profile is at its best in the morning. Photograph taken at 8.30 a.m. GMT on 6 March.

(Right) This right-facing head—pre-dating by thousands of years known sculptures of the Green Man—is one of Avebury's best heads, and very difficult to find. It is on Stone 206, in the North Circle, facing south-south-east. Photographed at 10.20 a.m. GMT on 26 November.

If it is the work of man, and not the chance juxtaposition of irregular surfaces, it is a masterpiece of execution, involving the dressing and merging of an array of contours. Sunshine brings the stone to life and provides the shadow to set off the right eye satisfactorily; this means about 9.00 to 11.00 a.m. GMT, 10.00 to 12 noon BST.

re-erection. East of Stone 210, at the northern edge of Green Street, is a standing fragment which is likely to be part of *Stone 209*. Dr Stukeley drew this as a fallen stone but subsequently part of it became the chimney-corner of a cottage since demolished. *Stone 222*, which Stukeley saw upright next to the east side of the Swindon road, was smashed up in about 1825. Its hundreds of pieces now make up the hedge-topped wall which bounds the road at that point. Stones 202 and 204 Stukeley recorded

William Stukeley's view from a position east-north-east of the Cove and the North Circle.
In front of the two Cove stones (B) stands Stone F. A little to the right is Stone G, and
farther again is Stone 222 by the side of the road. Extreme right but much nearer is Stone
201 (it is still there). Next to it is the fallen Stone 202, and in the foreground William Stukeley
depicts himself leaning against Stone 204. At the left is Stone 206 which is also present and
standing.

as fallen but they have since disappeared, together with other stones of this circle which
were reclining in his time. As for the surviving Type B *Stone 201*, three left-profile
heads, two of them faint, are visible on the south side at various times in late-afternoon
sunshine (3 to 5 p.m. BST).

A marvellous stone is *Stone 206* and we must be thankful for its survival. It has a
great head which is turned to 106 degrees east of north, the direction of the early-
February and early-November sunrises. Visible all year round, the right side of the

face is at its best in early morning sunshine, at which time the corresponding left side of the same face shows up well, too. Best of all, perhaps, is 9 to 10.30 a.m. winter time, after which the right eye is less good. The fine mouth is surely deliberately carved.

Beneath this head is another right-sided one facing the same way. This is visible at around 9–10 a.m. GMT, 10–11 a.m. BST, and perhaps longer, but *only* when the sun is shining. It has an appeal to it, like the Sun God Apollo or perhaps the Green Man. For a while both heads can be seen together as a parent-child combination. The sculptors probably took advantage of natural formations here, but if not they showed great ingenuity.

On the opposite side of the stone is the peaceful countenance of a left-profile head facing the early-May sunset. If this is truly a stone-carving, it is so well executed that it may even record the profile of a particular individual—say, a grandmother or elder with a gentle hooked nose—who lived in Avebury at the time when the monument was in use, and is now seen by us as through a window into the past. Or is it the work of a skilful craftsman improving upon an accidental freak of nature which he had spotted? Either way, the result is impressive.

This sculpture, like dozens of others at Avebury, reveals how cunning was the craftsman's art. Viewed from the front there is nothing to see but bumpy lumps of grey-brown rock. Only when studied from the south-south-west, at right angles to the outline, does the profile appear. This extraordinary art-form was invented over 4,000 years ago and afterwards lost; it was a secret device for producing images which the initiated could worship, artistic works of which strangers would be unaware.

Inside the North Circle, and concentric with it, there may be another circle composed of 12 stones. William Stukeley sketched one such stone as definitely standing—the one now called Stone F—and five others lying on the south and west sides of the conjectured circle. The proposal by Ucko and his colleagues in 1991, that two of Stukeley's sketches show Stone G as standing on the northern perimeter of the 12-stone circle, appears to be correct, although Stukeley marked one of his plans with a note that a stone at this position was demolished in 1713. A discussion begun by Isobel Smith (1965) and pursued by Ucko and others, about the validity of Stukeley's statements and maps concerning the evidence for a 12-stone inner circle, remains unresolved although there is enough to suggest that he may yet be proved right.

The most enigmatic of Avebury's stones is the feature which since Stukeley's time has been called the *Cove*. In his book *Abury* he wrote:

The North Circle 'has that immense work in the center which the old Britons call a cove: consisting of three stones plac'd with an obtuse angle toward each other, and as it were, upon an ark of a circle . . . like the upper end of the cell at Stonehenge; being of the same use and intent, the adytum of this temple. I have often times admir'd and been astonish'd at its extravagant magnitude and majesty. It stands in the yard belonging to the inn. King Charles II, in his progress this way, rode into the yard, on purpose to view it.'

According to this, Stukeley did not invent the word 'cove' but somehow accredited it to 'the old Britons'.

Two of the Cove stones survive, standing where Stukeley saw them in 1719—one a broad, massive stone, the other tall and narrow—at the centre of the North Circle. But in Stukeley's day a third had recently been demolished. In his words: 'It fell down in 1713, as marked in the ground-plot. They told me it was full seven yards long, of the same shape as its opposite, tall and narrow. We measured this 17 foot above ground, 10 whole cubits; 7 foot broad, two and a half thick. These were the wings of this noble ellipsis.'

Together the three standing stones formed a setting directed at the most northerly rising of the sun, the point on the distant hill over which the sun peeks at the summer solstice. But it seems that before Stukeley's time the Cove had a fourth stone, which lay flat between the others. Walter Charleton reported seeing it a few decades earlier, in the 1660s.

Dr Charleton's map, dated 8 July 1663, is a schematised and simplified restoration of the monument to which many missing stones have been introduced. He describes the fourth Cove stone as 'a Triangular stone, of vast magnitude, lying flat on ye ground; but, (probably) at first imposed on ye heads of ye other three in manner of an Architrave'.

Ucko and his colleagues have examined this and related questions in depth. A more likely alternative to its being an overhead stone is that the triangular stone was intended to lie flat on the ground just as Aubrey and Charleton found it. To have stood safely upon the other three, in the manner of Pentre Ifan in Wales, its dimensions would have exceeded the vast area between the three, so it could hardly have lain flat between them after falling. Ucko and his colleagues (1991: 235) reported an inspection by Michael Allen of the top surfaces of the surviving stones, and concluded that a capstone never stood upon them. It is commonplace in fertility religions for a triangle to symbolise the feminine gender. The same applies to broad massive stones like the centre Cove stone as seen from the determining direction which is that of the midsummer sunrise. By contrast, its companion stones betray masculine characteristics whose presence as 'male attendants' could be held to augment the power of the female stone between them—like the lions or lionesses which flank Goddesses in Cretan and Mycenean art.

The surviving Cove stones make a right angle (not an obtuse angle) to one another, and the direction which the Cove faces is that of the midsummer sunrise, 50 plus or minus 2 degrees, over Hackpen Hill in the distance.

The Cove does not face the most northerly moonrise as H. A. W. Burl claims (1979) (he gives 40 plus or minus 5) in his paper in the *Wiltshire Archaeological Magazine*

Avebury's North Circle. On the side of Stone 206 opposite the male heads is this left-sided visage of what may be an elderly woman or deity. Visible at any time of day, afternoon shadows heighten the power given to it by the tooling of the sculptor. Photographed at 2.20 p.m. GMT, 3.20 BST, on 29 April.

Regarding the distant stones of the South Circle is this right-sided face on Stone 7 (below left). Photographed at 8.30 a.m. GMT, 9.30 BST, on 25 October.

Stone 10 (below right) in the south-west quadrant. The head is seen in left-profile, facing south-west, as viewed edge-on from the south-east. This photograph was taken at 8.00 a.m. BST on 14 April.

Is it a frog? Is it a seal? Is it a mythical beast? This is Avebury's Stone 14, south-west quadrant. Photographed at 3.20 p.m. GMT on 21 January.

(Opposite) Four views of the great cove stone at Avebury, showing four of the five left-facing heads. From top left to bottom right they gaze, respectively, in the direction of: a) midwinter sunset (S corner viewed from the SE at 8.50 a.m. GMT, 9.50 BST); b) midwinter sunset (SE side viewed from the SE at 2.30 p.m. GMT, 3.30 BST); c) midsummer sunrise (N corner viewed from the NW); and d) midsummer sunset (E corner viewed from the NE at 11.00 a.m. GMT, 12 noon BST).

Outer Stone II. This fertility-cult stone in the hills next to the Ridgeway lies on the same May Day alignment as Female Stone 106 and the Obelisk. The triangular-topped megalith has a shallow groove along its middle in the tradition of yoni-honouring societies elsewhere. The red coloration is caused by algae living in the water-filled hollow.

Three left-sided images on Stone 98 at the southern entrance to the henge. Two face west, one above the other as if mother and daughter. The lower one was photographed at 8.40 a.m. GMT on 25 October; the upper one at 4.00 p.m. BST, 3.00 GMT, on 14 August. The most impressive head, possibly representing a priestess, faces east and was photographed at 7.00 p.m. BST, 6.00 GMT, on 31 March.

Avenue Stone 37b. Like a knight in a game of chess this 'horse's head' is known to all visitors. Photographed at 8.00 a.m. GMT, 25 October.

When viewed from the north it becomes a human head in left profile facing the midsummer sunrise. Photographed at 7.15 a.m. BST, 6.15 GMT, on 18 April.

Avenue Stone 31a has a good left-side representation of a head facing west, which can be seen in the afternoon sunshine on the southern end of the stone. About 3.00 p.m. BST, 2.00 GMT, the right-hand sides of a second and third face appear within the same zone as the first but facing the opposite way! Truly a virtuoso work of art. Photographed on 22 September at 3.40 p.m. BST, 2.40 GMT.

(Left) At West Kennet Long Barrow the carved head of a sheep facing left – logically a ewe – is evident at the base of Stone 25. Before the long barrow was sealed in the Late Neolithic era, the image was illuminated by the rising sun every March.

(Opposite) Four of the left-facing heads at West Kennet Long Barrow: Stones 31, 35, 36 and 46. The photograph of 46 was taken at midday on 13 July.

The right-profile face on the Heel Stone at Stonehenge is illuminated by the rising sun only in the week of the midsummer solstice, when the stone's male role is most obvious.

When viewed from the opposite side as the midsummer sun rises, the right profile of the stone appears in left profile.

The Cove at the centre of Avebury's North Circle. Two of its stones remain, one an obviously male stone, the other female. The female stone displays five heads, all left-facing, at various times of the day. This photograph was taken at 10.45 a.m. GMT (on 26 November) when the left eye, nose, mouth and ear of the great head show up well. Best times for watching are 10.30 to 11.30 a.m. GMT, 11.30 to 12.30 BST.

in 1988. Nor does it face the May sunrise (which would be 62–63 degrees) as proposed by Michael Dames. The latter went on to surmise that the North Circle was intended for male adolescents who had processed to it from the Beckhampton Avenue, going to a May Wedding; their 'sacred marriage' was consummated with maidens in the South Circle who had arrived from along the Kennet Avenue.

Proof that the broad centre stone or 'Goddess Stone' generally faces the midsummer sunrise is verified by standing at the north-west side of the megalith and checking the compass bearing of the uneven north-eastern face which is 140 plus or minus 2 degrees true, and then subtracting 90 degrees. This gives 50 plus or minus 2 degrees. The sunrise direction at the latitude of Neolithic Avebury is about 51½ for the horizon formed by Hackpen Hill. The effect of changes in the inclination of the ecliptic, at the rate of 0.2 degree per thousand years, in the 4,500 years since then, has increased the bearing by almost a further degree, to beyond 52 degrees.

The likelihood that the Cove's centre stone was a Goddess Stone is raised by the fact that there are no less than five left-profile heads on it.

The head low down on the north-eastern side is always visible, awaiting the midsummer sunrise and the fertilising power of the Cosmic Marriage—very like the female South Circle stones in combination with the sun and the male Obelisk. But the other heads require the sun to cast shadows at optimum angles.

Head 2 is on the narrow south-eastern side, visible in sunshine between 4 and 5 p.m., and turned towards the midwinter sunset. The next two are on the south-western side. Head 3, with its well-formed left eye, cheek, nose, and mouth, needs bright sunshine towards 8.30–9.00 p.m. GMT, 9.30–10.00 BST. It too faces the exact midwinter sunset. Head 4 faces north-west, and is truly visible only between 10.30 and 11.30 a.m. GMT or 11.30–12.30 BST daily. At this morning hour the sunlight transforms an innocuous hollow into a big eye; an impression of an ear follows, and the stone is again alive. For an hour or more, on every morning of the year when the sun is out, the awesome left eye and ear animate the otherwise unnoticed profile of nose, mouth and chin. Can the hollow that makes the eye be artificial? It gazes towards midsummer sunset over Windmill Hill. The fifth head, which looks to the midwinter sunrise, involves the eastern edge of the north-east side of the stone and appears around 8 to 9 in the morning. All four solsticial rising and setting points of the sun are represented among the five left-profile heads.

The arrangement of the Cove stones in relation to Stone F and the sunrise is broadly similar to that of each of the 15 stones of the South Circle in relation to the rising sun and the Obelisk. In the next chapter we shall see that a second cove, at Beckhampton, is designed in the same way, but directed towards the midwinter sunrise. It is also important to remember that the idea is repeated in principle at Stonehenge, where the internal U-settings correspond to Avebury's cove settings, as Stukeley first noticed so astutely in 1722–24! Megalithic U-settings in Britain correspond symbolically to yoni-shaped and womb-shaped temples in India. Instead of a U, British writers on Stonehenge sometimes choose the word horseshoe. It makes no difference: the reason why horseshoes became a universal door charm was because of yoni symbolism—the fertility-linked vulva shape—and the same goes for the cranium and upward horns of a bull.

A possible interpretation for the Avebury Cove, as I have already proposed for Stonehenge, is that the summer solstice commemorated the original Consummation of the Gods when the world was created. The intention is yearly fertilisation during a visual re-enactment of the Marriage which everyone could witness: the sun's rays penetrate the Earth Mother's genital shrine or womb (the stone circle) to arrive at a focal stone which is the centre female stone at Avebury's North Circle Cove, or the misnamed Altar Stone at Stonehenge.

Such occasions would have been joyous events in the lives of the worshippers. The festival may have lasted a couple of days or more, to give enough time for a grand celebration and to allow for the arrival of a sunrise of clear sky.

By contrast Dr Burl sees the Avebury Cove as a dark ritual construction mimicking a mortuary house, while the stone circle is simply 'a circular enclosure'; he declares that 'the rites with human bones that began here may have been completed elsewhere, perhaps in the adjacent South Circle' (Burl, 1979).

He continues by saying that the two coves 'themselves in the likeness of tomb entrances, were connected with the night', adding 'the North Circle with its Cove was possibly the place for winter rituals when the dead had offerings brought to them in the "forecourt" of the Cove itself' (Burl, 1979).

Yes, these coves are so like the entrances of long chambered mounds around Avebury that it is feasible that the coves were raised as imitations of those forecourts—the coves possibly constructed at the time when the chambered barrows were closed down. The first antiquarian to remark on close similarities between cove types at various stone monuments was William Stukeley in 1722–24. He specifically described a cove as signifying the 'great gate of the gods' (see Ucko and colleagues, 1991: 231; Stukeley, 1722–24)), and his generalised scheme of covelike settings embraced quoit-like structures, like Kits Coty in Kent and the previously mentioned interior U-settings at Stonehenge.

Subsequent scholars assume that death, mortuary deeds, bone-portage and ancestor honouring were the usual practices at these covelike arrangements (that is, at true coves, barrows, quoits and, for some, the Stonehenge interior). But while accepting some of these (*especially* the honouring of ancestors), I strongly believe that concepts of rebirth, life after death, fertility, myths of creation and the eternal return, and the solar penetration of the Earth Goddess's domain motivated the rites. The South Circle of stones was the genital shrine of fertility; the North Circle with cove was the genital shrine of creation. As at Stonehenge, the midsummer festival was the chief event of the year at Avebury, and the reason for building the North Circle cove. The midwinter festival was recognised at both great sites, but to judge by the stones it was a lesser event than the summer one for the people of ancient Wiltshire.

At Stonehenge the construction ensures that the midsummer sun rises clear of the Heel Stone, and then hides behind it. Fertilisation by the sun is followed by union with the phallic shadow of the Heel Stone, the penis-shaped megalith which may be the Sky Father's representative on earth. Full details will be found in *Stonehenge: The Secret of the Solstice.*

Two of the three left-facing heads noticed on Stone 201 of the North Circle. The whole stone was photographed at 10.20 a.m. GMT, on 26 November; the edge was photographed at 4.00 p.m. GMT, 5.00 BST, 25 August.

A related device seems to have been arranged at Avebury's North and South Circles and at Beckhampton Cove. On several sunrise dates at the South Circle the sun rises behind the Obelisk which, again, may have been the Sky Father's embodiment on Earth, and that interlithic shadow-casting took part in, or completed, the fertilisation process. It could be the same at the North Circle where, however, the construction is devoted to a single sunrise, at the summer solstice. The exact position of the stone-hole made for Stone F is not known, but to judge by the sketches of William Stukeley, by the plan of Isobel Smith (1965), by the subsurface geophysical survey reported by Ucko and colleagues (1991, Plate 68), and by direct observation of the existing turf-hollow, it seems that *Stone F used to stand either directly in front of the Cove or just slightly farther to the east.*

Because the Cove was built to face the midsummer rising sun in the Late Neolithic era, the first alternative would suggest that the sun used to rise directly behind Stone F, so that the day of the solstice began with the lower part of the middle Cove stone suffused with the shadow of Stone F. I have arrived at this judgement by estimating the height of Stone F, using Stukeley's sketches, and allowing for its distance and small altitude difference compared with the middle Cove stone. Stone F is therefore the Sky Father's personification on earth, and its shadow is the fertilising power.

With the second alternative the sun's first rays shine past Stone F to impregnate the whole of the middle Cove stone, soon after which the sun is eclipsed and fertilising shade takes the place of the sun on the lower part of the megalith only (as at Stonehenge; see *Stonehenge: The Secret of the Solstice*).

It is possible that hill-stones were arranged to serve the cove of the North Circle as it seems they were for megaliths of the South Circle. Contenders are (a) the grey sarsen on Totterdown by the Ridgeway, as suggested in chapter 4 when searching for Outer Stone I (whose bearing from the Cove is almost 52 degrees east of north), or a conglomerate-flint megalith 80–90 metres (90–100 yards) north of this stone at 51 degrees east of north; (b) a stone pair SU 1173 6884 at 51 degrees east of south, removed earlier this century; and perhaps (c) the lost stone on the south-east side of Windmill Hill whose bearing from the Cove was about 51 degrees west of north. Remember that the various heads on the principal Cove stone face the four solsticial risings and settings.

9

MIDWINTER FESTIVAL
Beckhampton Cove and Avenue

In 1722 William Stukeley saw the cove at Beckhampton in a damaged condition but more complete than it is today. There was also evidence of a stone avenue joining Beckhampton with the henge and circles of Avebury.

'This Longstone cove, vulgarly call'd long stones, is properly a cove, as the Britons call'd 'em, compos'd of three stones, like that most magnificent one we described, in the center of the northern temple at Abury; behind the inn. They are set upon the ark of a circle, regarding each other with an obtuse angle. This is set on the north side of the avenue; one of the stones of that side makes the back of the cove . . . It stands on the midway of the length of the avenue, being the fiftieth stone. This [cove] opens to the south-east, as that of the northern temple to the north-east . . . Dr Musgrove mentions it in his Belgium Britannicum, page 44 and in his map thereof. Mr Aubry . . . speaks of them by the name of the Devil's coits. Three huge stones then standing. It was really a grand and noble work. The stone left standing is 16 feet high, as many broad, 3½ thick. The back stone is fallen flat on the ground, of like dimension.'

The 'stone left standing' is the Cove stone, still there, which locals call Adam. The neighbouring megalith is a stone of the lost Beckhampton Avenue, which goes under the name Eve. Stukeley probably knew this because he labelled them A and E respectively. The back stone he called Stone B, and the next (missing) one Stone D.

Longstone Cove at Beckhampton is 1.3 km (¾ mile) west-south-west of Avebury, and seems to have been built to await the winter solstice sunrise. William Stukeley's reconstruction showed it to be a three-stone cove (that is, Stones A, B, D) with a fourth stone, C, set squarely before it, a little more than the width of the avenue separating B from C. The central megalith, Stone B, was drawn as a broad female stone, with A and D standing at obtuse angles at its sides. Both these 'companion stones' A and D have a decidedly angular, arguably feminine, allure, and since A (or 'Adam') is still there it is easy to check this! 'Adam' is indeed female, so if Stukeley's sketch is to be trusted, all three adjacent cove stones (A, B, D) were Keiller Type B female stones, suggesting a Goddess trinity. The opposing megalith C, however, is shown round-topped and was possibly a stone of the male gender.

By calculating the orientation we can claim that Beckhampton Cove opens to the near horizon in the vicinity of 130 degrees east of north. An exact estimate may not be possible until the holes of B and D have been excavated. However, Stone E is a stone of the Avenue to which the missing stone B would have been set parallel, and as E is perpendicular to 130 degrees east of north, so presumably was Stone B. The position of C (or its burning or burial pit) was revealed in the subsurface geophysical survey reported by Ucko and his colleagues (1991: 196–9 and Plate 63) which shows C as being 12 metres (40 feet) south-south-east of A.

Either at sunrise *or soon after*, the shadow of Cove Stone C would fall upon the centre Stone B, depending upon whether the drama was intended to duplicate that of Avebury's South Circle stones or Stonehenge's Heel and Altar Stones (which may be the same as Avebury's North Circle Cove although this is yet to be proved). Either way, Sacred Marriage between Heaven and Earth, or Sky Father and Earth Mother, could explain this arrangement as being that of the New Year Story. This is the turning point of the dead season when the shortest day is marked and joy is released as the New Year is honoured. Aided by ritual and prayer, the days would henceforth lengthen, and life would return as the rural year began anew. At the start of February the ewes would be in milk (Celtic Imbolc); after the equinox the days would be longer than the nights and the spring lambs would leap and run; and at the start of May the summer vegetation would flower, and youthful human life would be exuberant. Celebrating the winter solstice was a notable event in the calendar; it gave reassurance that the year was on the turn.

Stukeley estimated that the Cove was sited 50 megalith-pairs west of the entrance to Avebury Henge. Six avenue stones appear in his cove sketch. His other pictures reveal more stones, several lying at intervals along Avebury's High Street. Counting every avenue stone in Stukeley's plans, the total exceeds 30. Some are shown as opposite pairs.

Included among the stones of the High Street were two, to use Stukeley's words, 'by the parsonage-gate on the right hand' and one that 'now lies at the corner of the next house, on the right hand, by the lane turning off to the right, to the bridge. Another was broke in pieces to build that house with, anno 1714. Two more lie on the left

The surviving megalith of Beckhampton Cove is an angular Type B stone. In the distance is the sole survivor of the Beckhampton Avenue that is still standing.

hand, opposite. It then passes the beck, south of the bridge. Most of the stones hereabouts have been made use of about the bridge, and the causeway leading to it.'

In 1879 Bryan King published his observation that very large sarsens had been used for making this causeway and the foundations of the bridge itself. He records that a stone at the corner of the parsonage premises had been broken up within the memory of a man recently deceased (Smith, 1965: 217). Some confirmation of Stukeley's comments came in the late 1960s when a burning pit was seen during road works in the High Street.

Dr Stukeley continues: 'Now the avenue passes along a lane to the left hand of the

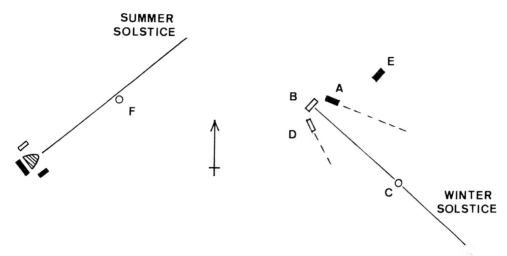

(Left) The cove at Avebury awaiting midsummer sunrise. The base of the cove was provided with a stone floor in the form of a huge triangular flat sarsen. The best estimate for Stone F's location is indicated, but its exact position can only be clarified by excavation.
(Right) Reconstruction of the Beckhampton Cove, after Stukeley, and the direction of midwinter sunrise. The position of Stone C was confirmed by the geophysical surveying work reported by P. Ucko and his colleagues.

Caln road, by a stone house call'd Goldsmiths-farm, and so thro' farmer Griffin's yard, thro' one barn that stands across the avenue, then by another which stands on its direction. Two stones and their opposites still lie in the foundation; immediately after this, it enters the open plow'd fields; the Caln road running all the while north of it. If we look back and observe the bearings of Abury steeple, and other objects, a discerning eye finds, that it makes a great sweep or curve northwards. The avenue entering the open corn-fields, runs for some time by the hedge, on the right hand. When it has cros'd the way leading from South-street, we discern here and there the remains of it, in its road to Longstone cove. Farmer Griffin broke near 20 of the stones of this part of the avenue.'

Here Stukeley relates that Cove Stone D was broken by fire by Richard Fowler, that 20 cartloads were needed to bear it away, and that in the stone were perfect flints and, in the middle, petrified bones. Stuckeley speaks of seeing such a fragment 'in a garden-wall of the little ale-house below in Beckhampton-road, which evidently had a bone in it'.

One may wonder why the sites of so few stones were detected in the course of the subsurface geophysical work of Ucko and his colleagues. One possibility is that, apart from the Cove and the stones in its vicinity, the Avenue's megaliths were smaller than average, and the stone-holes also (especially if the Avenue was built early or very late in the history of Avebury's construction era). This could explain why the stones of this avenue were rooted out earlier and more efficiently than elsewhere. If the holes were shallow, and their apparent depth further reduced by chalk dissolution over four thousand years (Richard Atkinson suggests there has been a loss of 50 cm (20ins) of subsurface chalk), or were refilled with chalk rubble, their presence would be hard to detect. I have previously suggested that a similar situation may exist in the Stonehenge Avenue which might have been lined by the smaller bluestones when they were withdrawn from Stonehenge for a part of the 26th-century BCE (see *Stonehenge: The Secret of the Solstice*, p. 116).

Moving on from the Cove, Stukeley writes, 'A little way hence . . . is a great barrow, call'd Longstone long barrow' and the Avenue passed by it on the east side. 'Three stones lie still by the field-road coming from South-street to the Caln-road. Mr Alexander told me he remember'd several stones standing by the parting of the roads under Bekamton, demolish'd by Richard Fowler.'

Stukeley's Plate XXIV shows some of these stones; in the distance is South Street Long Barrow being crossed by the track called Nash Road or South Street.

In 1950 W. E. V. Young reported that a buried sarsen was struck when ploughing. Investigation revealed that a child had been buried alongside, together with a beaker pot, the bones of a bull, and a piece of chalk artificially inscribed with deep grooves.

In 1968, when the Post Office was digging a pipe trench alongside the A4 Bath Road, Faith and H. L. Vatcher saw a large sarsen buried in a pit cut into the chalk (SU 0875.6899), which is on or close to the line of the Avenue as illustrated by Stukeley (*Abury* 35–6, Tab. XXIV). This was just west of the A4 roundabout, while seven metres (23 feet) farther west another depression appeared to mark the site of another buried stone.

Stukeley's drawings indicate a few more stones south-west of the London-Bristol road on a continuation of the avenue line. He concludes by supposing that the avenue continued farther into the fields, as far as a point near the Roman road and a group of barrows under Cherhill, from which 'very point only you can see the temple on Overton-hill', that is the Sanctuary. O. G. S. Crawford in 1922 wondered whether 'on the north side of the Devizes Road at the corner of the field 120 feet ENE of spot-level 506 an upright sarsen stone (was) possibly connected with the Avenue'. Unfortunately the stone had gone long before 1998.

10

AN AVENUE OF FACES
The Kennet Avenue, the Sanctuary, and Falkner's Circle

South and east from Avebury runs Kennet Avenue, Britain's finest double stone row. Before its almost total destruction, it was 2.5 kilometres (1½ miles) long, and linked the stone circles of Avebury with the Overton Hill circles which William Stukeley had named the Sanctuary.

When it was complete, the Avenue consisted of about one hundred pairs of stones, and there were about 60 more stones at the Sanctuary. Today all the Sanctuary stones are missing, and the majority of Avenue stones have gone too. The section of the Avenue that we admire so much in the northern third of its course is there only because of the conscientious restoration work of Alexander Keiller, which he undertook from 1934 to 1936.

I have used here the stone-numbering system followed by Isobel Smith in her report on Keiller's excavations. The numbering begins at the Avebury end. Stones of a pair are indicated by the letters 'a' and 'b', 'a' meaning a stone on the left side of the avenue, and 'b' a stone on the right. Therefore the more northerly and easterly stone of a pair is called Stone a, and the more southerly and westerly one is Stone b.

Before Keiller's work began, the only stones standing were numbers 4b and 21a alongside the road near Avebury, Stones 33a and 33b in the long field, Stones 52b

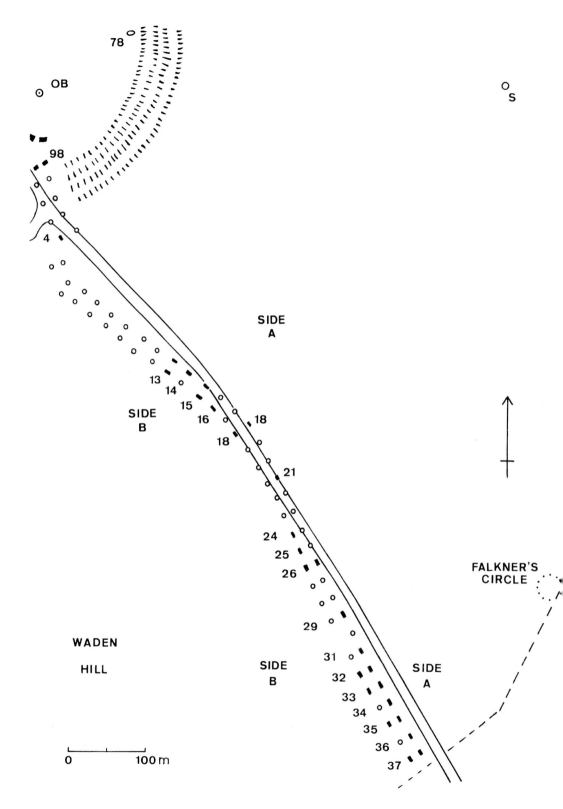

Kennet Avenue, northern section, showing sites of present and absent stones. The survivor of Falkner's Circle is also shown, as well as the position of a large sarsen S which has gone missing.

and 54b by the roadside halfway to West Kennet, and Stones 79b and 81b at West Kennet alongside the A4 Bath-London road. Stone 33a had been re-erected in 1912. Visible fallen stones in the northern sector were 31a, 32a, 32b, 34a, 35a, 35b, 36a, 37a, and 37b.

Isobel Smith records that thirteen deliberately buried stones were unearthed by Keiller: numbers 13a, 13b, 14a, 15a, 15b, 16b, 18a, 18b, 24b, 25b, 26a, 26b, and 29a. Stone 19b was there as a fallen stone but had become hidden beneath an accumulation of soil.

The megaliths outside the southern entrance of the henge fell, or were felled, centuries ago. John Aubrey was informed by Walter Sloper, Attorney, of Munkton, about the fall of one which led him to insert a note in his unpublished manuscript: '. . . the great stone at Aubury's Townsend, where this Walke begins, fell down in Autumn 1684, and broke in two or three pieces: it stood only (two) foot deep in the earth' (Fowles and Legg, p. 37). This could have been *Stone 1a* or *Stone 1b*.

Just outside the henge bank a sad fragment of *Stone 3a* can be seen. Then, across the road is the first undamaged standing stone, *Stone 4b*. It has a hunched, bison-like appearance—best appreciated in good sunshine about 3 p.m. GMT (4 p.m. BST) by viewing its western or left side—and is of a bulk that seems fitting for one of the guardian or 'welcoming' stones. At its northern end a good representation of the left side of a human head appears out of the shadows a little later in the afternoon while the right side of this head remains in the shade. At its southern end, a left-sided head faces down the avenue in late morning and a right-sided head faces down the avenue at around midday.

After this there is a long gap devoid of megaliths, a space of land which was occupied earlier this century by allotments and fowl-runs.

Stones 13a and 13b are the first paired stones whose shapes imply sexual opposites. Stone 13b is a female lozenge with a left-profile head looking south. It is at its best before 7 a.m. BST in the summer; the stone may also have a 'midday' left-profile head on its opposite side looking north. The tall Stone 13a is a masculine pillar whose surfaces are much damaged but may display a right-profile head around 7 a.m. BST in the summer. (See p. 4 for a photograph of these stones.)

Stone 14a is small and squat (a Keiller Type B stone) with a left-view head facing north near midday.

Stone 15a is a cracker because the entire stone can be interpreted as a standing figure! Although this is visible all day, you can take the best photographs at midday. Because it is in left profile it suggests a female figure. Its companion stone (*15b*) is a tall, masculine pillar. On its western edge facing north-west a head is visible, with difficulty, in mid-afternoon sunshine.

Next is *Stone 16b* near the roadside hedge. Its southern end needs to be viewed end-on when regarding the left edge. The left side of a head can then be seen facing west

(Above) Avenue Stone 4b stands like a bison or watchdog just south of the henge, looking back at the entrance. This photograph was taken at 1.30 p.m. GMT on 14 December. Hidden in the shadow on the left is a good rendering of a human head which progressively emerges into sunlight after 3.00 p.m. GTM, 4.00 BST—as shown in the accompanying photograph.

(Right) One of the heads which is in shadow above is reproduced in this photograph (taken at 2.50 p.m. GMT, 3.50 BST, on 23 October).

Avenue Stone 14a, a tubby little stone seen from the west at 12.30 p.m. BST, 11.30 a.m. GMT, on 27 April.

if the time of day is midday, say 12 BST or 11 GMT. The same head can also be seen from its right-hand side.

Stone 18b, of more or less female-lozenge shape, stands alongside the roadside fence. A left-profile head faces north (midday sunshine is best). A disturbed oval grave only three feet long was found cut into the chalk on the north-east side of the stone, separated from the stone-hole by a ridge of chalk 12cm (4ins) wide. Isobel Smith (1965: 209) suggests that the body was probably male. Its companion stone is a small but narrow male pillar (*Stone 18a*) which stands on the opposite side of the road but may be much reduced in size.

The next stone has a cleverly carved head pecked into its southern edge. This is *Stone 19b,* just inside the field boundary. Its left-profile head shows up quite well

Avenue Stone 15a. A female angular stone with the image of the left side of a standing figure. Its companion stone, 15b, is a typical male pillar. Photographed at 12.30 p.m. BST, 11.30 a.m. GMT, on 27 April.

(Right) Kennet Avenue. The southern end of Stone 16b photographed at midday in the summer.

(Below) Side view of a well-defined head on Avenue Stone 19b. This megalith used to be a polishing stone. Near its base on the north-east side are three narrow grooves suggestive of arrow-head sharpening and an oval area smoothed and hollowed by the repeated polishing of axe-heads. Photographs taken at 10.10 a.m. BST, 9.10 GMT, on 27 August.

(Left) Avenue Stone 26a. The east side of the entire megalith has been made into a right-sided head—a procedure which seems to have involved a considerable amount of surface dressing. It is a Keiller Type A, male stone, and its companion a whitish Type B angular stone. The great head is seen at its best when lit by the sun in the early morning. Photograph taken at 7.00 a.m. BST, 6.00 GMT, on 18 April.

(Right) Avenue Stone 26b. This female lozenge-type stone faces south down the Kennet Avenue. Photographed at 8.00 a.m. GMT, 25 October.

towards sunset in winter (about 4 p.m. GMT) but it can probably be appreciated at any time on a sunny afternoon. This includes viewing the face from its front, or from the south, as well.

There is a second head in left profile occupying the north side of the stone. This stone was used for tool-polishing before it became part of the Avenue. Low down on its east side but angled to it are three V-shaped grooves 105 to 130mm (4 to 5ins) long, 10–15mm (⅜–½in) broad and up to 12mm (½in) deep, of a type that comes from sharpening flint or stone tools or weapons. Next to these is a smoothed oval area 280mm (11ins) long, 130mm (5ins) broad, and 20mm (¾in) deep in the middle, the result of much grinding. For this type of wear to be achieved the megalith would have lain flat for many years. It is the second-best polissoir known for Stone Age Britain.

To look at the next monolith, in correct order, cross the road again. This is the 20-ton *Stone 21a* on the other side of the highway. There appears to be a star-gazing left-profile head which is formed by the uppermost surfaces of this stone. When photographs taken around midday in April and August are turned on their sides, the head, with a left eye, nose and mouth, can be seen gazing at the northern half of the sky. Although *Stone 22b* has been taken away, an oval grave 4½ feet by 4 feet 1 inch was found on its north-east side. A male skeleton lay on its back with the head to the west and feet to the east. The head was turned to the right or south, and the legs were drawn up but not tightly bent.

Stone 24b is very damaged, so despite its interesting outline (probably a lozenge before it was broken) all we can say about it is that there may be a left-profile head looking southwards and a yoni or vulva at ground level on the south side. The triangular-topped whitish *Stone 25b* is the one which Keiller and Piggott thought had an artificial cup-and-ring mark on its western face, but the mark is natural. Higher on the same face are two impressed rings which may also be natural but may help to explain the choice of megalith by the Avebury people. On the north-eastern side a prehistoric skeleton was found, but part of it was lost when the stone was buried in recent centuries. Altogether, three corpses had been buried at this place, and a beaker as well, but the site has been much disturbed.

Stones 26a and b are another typical A-B pair, 26a being Type A (male, pillar-like) and 26b being Type B (female, rhomboid-shaped). Appropriately, Stone 26a carries a huge impression of a right-sided head which the theory of gender-handedness rates as masculine. This is best seen in the early morning sunshine.

Stone 29a is of the female-lozenge type. A forward-looking face on its western side (two eyes and a mouth) is a natural feature of the rock which the Neolithic people may have liked. The left side of a head on its southern end faces south. Another Beaker grave had been placed on the stone's north-eastern side, probably of an adult male. Stones 29b and 30a are among those missing, but Stone 30b was never set in place. Keiller searched carefully for the stone-hole and came to the conclusion that such a stone was never raised. It has been suggested that this area was an occupation site, whereas I favour the possibility of a cult site or shrine. Michael Dames (1977) wondered whether the completion of 29-and-a-half pairs of stones corresponded to the moon's monthly cycle of the same number of days. Keiller, in searching for the missing stone, uncovered in the general area from Stone 27 to Stone 32 two ritual pits and ten smaller holes, all containing dark soil mixed with charcoal. An abundance of worked flints, especially near the missing Stone 30b, showed that there had been intense activity thereabouts.

Viewed from inside the avenue, *Stone 31a* falls in the Type B class. When its southern edge is lit by the sun in the south-west or west, a left-profile head facing west appears. This is easy to see for only two to three hours in the afternoon. It is an extraordinary work of art, if it is deliberate and not accidental, because if you look carefully at around 3.30 p.m. BST when the sun is out, you will see a second head facing the opposite way.

Stone 32a is a badly-damaged Type B stone strengthened by non-corrosive repair rods which affect its appearance. There may have been an east-facing head before the stone was mutilated, but the left-profile head at the north-western lower corner is probably unintended. Its whitish companion *Stone 32b* is a Type A pillar-like stone.

Stone 33b is a big Type B megalith, weighing about 15 tons, with traces of a face and big mouth (but no eye) on its southern end facing south. A sky-facing left-profile head can be seen from the west starting around 11 a.m. BST. No certain head has been spotted on 17-ton Type B *Stone 33a*, but a possible weathered left-profile head is visible on the northern side when viewed form the north-west at about 3.30 p.m. BST.

The next megaliths are *Stone 34a* and *Stone 35b*, both of the female-lozenge class. Perhaps carved heads were thought unnecessary because of the sexuality displayed by the lozenges, although 35b has a possible, but natural, vulva at the centre-bottom of its western side.

Stone 35a bears the image of what seems to be a left-profile face. As Michael Dames has said, it recalls the facial image on the Heel Stone at Stonehenge, while Paul Devereux (1992) asks whether it might be the Earth Goddess in one of her three aspects. In *The Avebury Cycle* Michael Dames proposed that its alignment to a pair of round barrows on the ridge of Avebury Down (measured as 50 degrees from north) corresponded with the midsummer sunrise, but the sun rises at 52½ degrees so could never have risen between the two barrows. The stone's face is, however, skewed roughly towards Silbury Hill which, although concealed by Waden Hill, lies on the same 050–230 alignment as Stone 35a and the twin barrows.

Stone 36a is most likely Type A because of the prominence given to the long semi-cylindrical mark which runs vertically down the middle of its eastern side, making it appear ithyphallic. This is the stone's only feature and probably its *raison d'être*. The right-profile head that appears around 8.30 a.m. in the summer, looking north up the avenue, is likely to be accidental, and there is another unlikely one facing west in the late afternoon sunshine.

The last stone-pair in the avenue is especially interesting. *Stone 37a* is a typical lozenge stone, but when viewed from the south in the early morning sun (say 9–11 a.m. BST, 8–10 GMT) a complete standing figure in left profile comes into sight. It shows up even better at 5–6 p.m. when the eye socket is stronger. Another left-facing head can be seen in the late morning. The main west-facing figure gazes at its companion stone (number *37b*) which has a left-profile animal-like head, like the horse-headed knight in a game of chess. Amazingly, when its northern edge is viewed edge-on

Avenue Stones 33b and 33a. Stone 33b is a star-gazer. Turn the photograph sideways to see the left-side of a head watching events in the sky. Visible for much of the morning, but best between 11 a.m. and 2 p.m. BST, 10 and 1 GMT. Photographed at 11.20 a.m. BST, 10.20 GMT, 18 October.

from the north in the early morning sunshine, a huge left-profile head, with well developed eye and nose, appears. The latter is turned towards the midsummer sunrise. This pair of stones is another female twosome, like pairs 33 and 35.

* * *

Of the 27 standing stones so far discussed, some of which are damaged, eight are

Kennet Avenue Stone 35a. This well-known head is turned to the midwinter sunset approximately. Photographed 25 November at 9.00 a.m. GMT.

Avenue Stone 36a. The hint of symbolic ithyphallicism renders this a male stone. It is best viewed in the morning. This photograph was taken at 10.20 a.m. BST, 9.20 GMT, on 10 September.

lozenge-shaped. Twenty-one appear to be Keiller Type B stones, and only six can be defined as male Type A, one of which (Stone 26a) displays a huge right-profile head while another (Stone 36a) in possessing a natural phallic-type mark has possibly one or two right-profile heads on it. In all, 16 left-side heads can be counted, as against a total of five right-side ones.

* * *

The next stones are about 370 metres (400 yards) to the south. In between, the sites of invisible stone positions from Stones 38 to 44 have been detected by subsurface geophysical measurements and reported by Ucko and colleagues in 1991. Locations for Stones 46 to 49 were possibly detected too, but after this the highway runs so close to the Avenue that it interferes with the detectors.

Stone 52b lies on the west side of the road towards West Kennet. From the west, its left side has a head facing north that could be human. *Stone 54b* is 50 metres (55 yards) to the south-east on the opposite side of the road; a possible head facing south-east shows up in the mid-afternoon sunshine.

Just before these stones is the region where Dr Stukeley guessed another cove may

Kennet Avenue, Stone 37a. Left-sided head and body facing Waden Hill to the west.
Photographed 18 July at 5.45 p.m. BST, 4.45 GMT.

have been sited (SU 1101 6881). Initially, because the Beckhampton Avenue has a cove at about the fiftieth stone as counted from Avebury, Stukeley searched for a similar cove on the Kennet Avenue using the same count. He was encouraged having read John Aubrey who wrote of a cove south of Avebury near (West) Kennet: 'Southward from Aubury in the ploughed field—near Kennet doe stand three huge stones perpendicularly, like the three stones at Aubury. They are called the Devill's Coytes.' It is unclear when John Aubury wrote this, but the same wording was later used in the 1695 edition of Camden's *Britannia*.

Many commentators think that through a memory lapse John Aubrey wrote 'south' and 'Kynet' although he had seen the cove to the west at Beckhampton. In order to be fair to Aubrey, Ucko and his team made a search by subsurface geophysical testing in this region, but with no result due to the proximity of the roadway. Only excavation may resolve this issue. However, on the basis of Stukeley's drawing of the Beckhampton Cove, if John Aubrey had seen this cove instead of the 'Kynet Cove', he might better have written of a group of five standing stones (A to E) of which three were adjacent Cove stones.

Farther on, in the field about 50 metres (55 yards) before the enclosure around the north side of the farm and 25 metres (27 yards) from the roadside (SU 1118 6856), the Ordnance Survey map published in 1924 recorded a stone which could be the one that O. G. S. Crawford had noted was being buried in the winter of 1921–22. Its location corresponds to Avenue Stone 63b (Smith, 1965: 207).

Stones 79b to 82b lie behind and in the hedge on the south side of the A4 road farther to the east than West Kennet House. A stile giving access to the field makes it possible to get a good view of them. *Stone 79b* is a broken standing stone with a triangular outline. *Stone 80b*, of Type B with possibly a left-profile head, lies fallen. The next stone (*81b*), two metres long and in the hedge, appears to be standing. The last visible megalith, *Stone 82b*, is of the angular B type but has fallen. Finally, *Stone 83b*, seen by A. D. Passmore in 1926, is now out of sight beneath an accumulation of soil. One hopes that before long the fallen stones will be raised and the hedge cut back to give a full view of all five stones. Lastly, Isobel Smith (1965: Plate 38a) provides a photograph of the small lozenge-type *Stone 77b* which in 1957 was allowed to remain *in situ* beneath the asphalt of the A4 main road.

Four additional megaliths are worth noting. One lies near a field-edge on the valley floor, easily accessible on National Trust land just outside the north fence of West Kennet Farm (SU 1125 6852). There is a hole through the megalith near one of its corners. This 2½-ton lichen-covered stone may have a left-profile head on it. The stone's location is within 20 metres (22 yards) of the estimated position of the nearest stone-hole, that of *Stone 66a*. Its size is about $1.5 \times 1.25 \times 0.5$ metre ($5 \times 4 \times 1½$ feet), which is not very different from that of Stone 77b. Not far off, on National Trust property at SU 1116 6845, is a roadside bank where several sarsens lie covered in soil.

Megalith by field edge at West Kennet a little to the north of the nearest part of the Kennet Avenue where Stone 66a used to be. Its weight is about $2^1/_2$ tons. At the left a small hole passes straight through the stone. Photographed at 9.00 a.m. BST, 8.00 GMT, on 4 May 1998.

Two weigh about 2.5 tons and are big enough to have been Avenue stones. The third is smaller, about one ton, and if raised again would be triangular-topped. On a medial line below the centre the stone appears to be completely pierced by a round hole 30mm (1¼ins) in diameter and at least 200mm (8ins) in length. The stone is 1.5 metres (5 feet) long, about the size of the smallest Avenue stones and typical of the Neolithic Sanctuary Stones as described by John Aubrey and William Stukeley.

Farther east, no other stones are known to remain between Stone 82b and the Sanctuary. A burning pit has been seen close to the estimated positions of Pairs 96 and 97, and soon after this we come to the Sanctuary (SU 118 679).

The Sanctuary is the monument which William Stukeley witnessed being destroyed by a farmer in 1723 and 1724 'to gain a little dirty profit'. John Aubrey had been there some 60–70 years earlier: 'on the brow of the hill, is another monument . . . a double circle of stones, four or five feet high, the most are now fallen down.' The hill is called Overton Hill, but Maud Cunnington who excavated the Sanctuary (1931) recorded that the locals favoured a different name, Kennet Hill. This is more likely to be the ancient name, and before that it would have been Cunnit Hill after the prehistoric name for the river.

The attack on these stones was so thorough that the site had become lost, until redis-

Rundway   *tr. rrid*   *Re. Camp*   *Silbury*   *Windmill boll*   *Abury*

William Stukeley's drawing of the Sanctuary shows two rings of sarsens which John Aubrey said were 4 to 5 feet high. Aubrey employed the word 'high' although he added that most of the stones had fallen down.

covered by Maud Cunnington in 1930 using Stukeley's sketches. In fact William Long on his map, published in the *Wiltshire Archaeological Magazine* in 1857, had placed the Sanctuary in exactly the right spot, at the field corner by the Ridgeway and the A4 main road. In this he was following John Aubrey who explained that the Sanctuary with its stones 'fower and five feet high' was 'on the brow of the hill above Kynet, on the right hand of the high way which goes from Bristow to Marleborough'. Maud Cunnington's excavations revealed that the monument had consisted of four rings of timber posts and two rings of sarsen stones. There had been 18 stones in the inner ring and 42 in the outer, and a couple more besides. Just inside the eastern stone of the inner circle was a grave with the remains of an adolescent and a beaker.

Stuart Piggott's study of the findings suggested that there had been three phases of

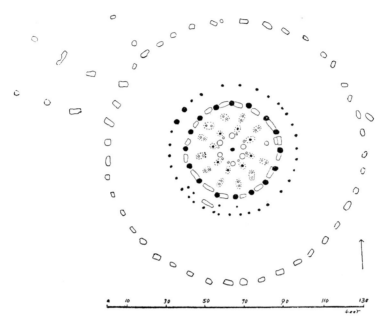

Maud Cunnington's excavation plan of the Sanctuary. Open symbols denote stone-holes, and closed symbols timber posts.

Small Circle near Kennet.   (Falkner, 1840.)

Plan of Falkner's Stone Circle as given in A. C. Smith's paper in 1885. In 1840 two stones lay fallen in addition to the standing one. North is not indicated but it is suspected that the shadow is pointing roughly west.

timber construction, probably in connection with the raising of a building of increasingly large diameter, and a fourth phase when the stone circles were introduced. Joshua Pollard in 1992 published a fresh appraisal of the evidence, arguing that the monument was constructed around 2500 BCE, plus or minus a hundred years, in one or at most two stages. He proposes that the Beaker burial alongside the eastern inner stone happened about five centuries later. Today, rings of low concrete stumps mark the positions of the stolen stones and decayed posts.

This was Stukeley's 'Temple on Overton Hill', which for a year or two he decided had been dedicated to the Goddess Ertha, 'the Mother Earth supposing she is particularly concerned in human affairs & goes from People to People' (1722–4b).

Where did the stones go? Mostly four to five feet high, they were small enough to be dragged away whole, in which case probably few were broken up and most still exist in the neighbourhood (chiefly in buildings, gardens, walls and under roads). Over a dozen good candidates have been spotted in the nearest villages, one of which was mentioned above in connection with a roadside bank at West Kennet Farm.

There is one more monument in the Valley of the Kennet Avenue which must have had special significance in the sacred geography of the complex Avebury landscape. This is *Falkner's Circle*, but all that remains is a single megalith at SU 1098 6931, about 260 metres (285 yards) north-east of Stone 33a of the Kennet Avenue. The stone weighs about 2 tons and stands only 1.25m (4ft) high.

William Long wrote in the *Wiltshire Archaeological Magazine* in 1858 that Mr Falkner of Devizes told him that he had seen a circle there in 1840. It comprised the one standing stone and two fallen ones, together 'with nine hollow places from which stones had been removed'. Both Stukeley and Aubrey had missed this. William Long gives a plan of the 12-stone circle, diameter about 36 metres (120 feet). In a letter Mr Falkner wrote that 'the circle was then in a meadow, which was broken up a few years afterwards, and two of the (fallen) stones removed'.

11

THE WOMB-TOMB OF THE GODDESS

Fertility image and mural heads at West Kennet Long Barrow

On rising ground south of Silbury Hill is West Kennet Long Barrow, one of Britain's best known chambered monuments. From it the Sanctuary can be seen, one-and-a-half kilometres (about a mile) to the east, but Avebury to the north is obscured by the vastness of Waden Hill. To the north-west is Swallowhead Spring, one of the sources of the tantalising River Kennet which in wet years flows fast below but in the drier weather of recent times has been desiccated for years on end.

The long barrow was constructed around the middle of the fourth millennium, current estimates being about 3600 BCE, and it is thought to have been closed around 2400 to 2300 BCE.

The stones of the barrow have subtle heads, too. Although faint ones can be seen outside under very good conditions, the best are inside and have never been subjected to weathering. For instance, opposite Stone 18, with its fluted section made by axe-grinding, is Stone 25, at whose base is *a cleverly crafted head of an animal, apparently a ewe, carved in relief and shown in left-facing profile.*

Much of the stone is a smooth, reddish sarsen with a pitted surface, but the section which has been worked, close to the ground, has a whiter hue. About an inch depth of stone was removed in order to achieve this picture in bas-relief.

The best head is found on the east-facing Stone 21 of the west chamber. This is a human head in relief and profile, its physical proportions exact in outline. It is one of the finest human heads in low relief known for the British Neolithic, and is nearly as accomplished as the best of the Avebury ones, although it is distinctly older.

Because left-facing profiles imply femininity, it is possible that this might be an icon of the divinity of the tomb-temple: *the Temple Goddess, so subtly carved that no one but the initiated—those who understood the world of the Neolithic Earth Goddess—would know it was there.*

The head is on the western wall, and because the sun rises in the east at the equinoxes there was a spring illumination by the rising sun for a thousand years or more before the blocking stones were set in place. This means that the carving could be the left-side profile of a Spring Fertility Goddess.

In her book *The Earth Goddess* Cheryl Straffon describes how *The Goddess of Winter, in the eternal round of the seasons, becomes the Goddess of Spring.* Knowledge of this pagan tradition makes one wonder whether Stone 22, which is the next mega-lith taken clockwise round the end cell of the tomb-temple, might represent in some manner the Goddess of Winter. This is difficult to answer because the stone has no obvious head like the others, yet there are indications that in the eyes of the believers it may have represented a left-profile skull instead. For instance, the stone has a round-topped cranium and on its left side a noticeable concavity, very similar to the nose-less hollow of a skull. Certainly this stone (like the Ewe's Head on Stone 25) would receive the pre-equinox mid-March sun before Stone 21 got the post-equinox late-March sun. If we are looking for symbols of young life, the discovery by Dr John Thurnam in 1859 of 'the chief part of the skull of an infant about a year old' is surely meaningful. It had been placed between the upright edges of Stones 21 and 22 in line with the gallery, and alongside the baby's delicate cranium lay a heap of sherds and three struck flakes of flint one of which, the excavator remarked, was transparent.

Together the three stones may tell a story.

The ewe's head is turned toward both stones, 22 and 21. Its presence calls to mind the Imbolc lambing-festival which falls in early February on our Roman calendar, the time when *oi-melg*, or ewe's milk, begins to flow, and was formerly taken as the Herald of Spring. A carving of a ewe may therefore be a symbol for spring. Because the equinoctial barrow faces east, the way in which the rays of the rising sun fall first on the 'skull' of Stone 22 before reaching the head on Stone 21 suggests that the transition from Winter Goddess to the Spring Goddess could have been planned into this mural sequence, and that what was being celebrated was an early version of the Rites of Spring.

The western cell in West Kennet Long Barrow has two heads on the end wall. At the left, on Stone 21, is a well-proportioned left-facing head with nose, eye, mouth, chin and ear, while the next stone, 22, has a shape suggesting a left-facing skull of death, with rounded cranium and absent nose. The shape of the back of the head on Stone 21 is angled steeply downward in the direction of the 'mouth' of the skull as if to suggest rebirth from the dead. On the ground between the megaliths by the dry-stone wall a human skull had been placed. The stones form part of a mural sequence of seven stones with left-facing heads which extends all along the northern side of the gallery and into the forecourt where there are two more. The Earth Goddess is summoning the springtime sun to accomplish the rebirth.

The decommissioning of the temple/tomb of what could be a Spring Goddess around 2400–2300 BCE may have given devotees mixed feelings—their sorrow or reluctance at doing so was tempered by the new manifestation of the spring festivals which they had devised at Avebury henge. Just as the Vulva Stone (Stone 106) of the South Circle corresponds to the May Fertility Festival, it is possible that another stone of Avebury's South Circle corresponded to the Herald-of-Spring sunrise and festival. For example, the sunrise bearing of the shadow-making Obelisk as seen from Stone 109 is 98 degrees, which is an early-March date; or the bearing of Stone 123 as viewed from the Obelisk is 89 degrees, effectively the same as the equinoctial gallery of the West Kennet long barrow.

These two carvings in the barrow appear to have been executed before the barrow was completed, about 3600 BCE. This makes them Britain's oldest datable mural art, and illustrates how advanced good British sculpture was.

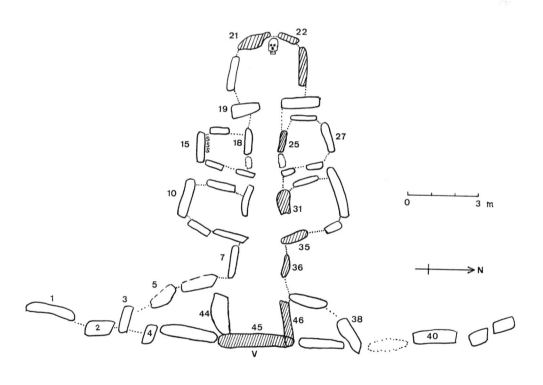

Plan of the standing stones at West Kennet Long Barrow (after S. Piggott). The nine stones with left-facing heads are shown hatched. Stone 45 is the megalith with vulva V on its east-facing side. SSS is where the three skulls lay in line.

When the barrow was under construction, the roof may have been left off for long enough to verify that the direction of the gallery allowed the east-rising March sunshine to reach the murals in the desired manner, for the best two images (on Stones 21 and 25) show up well when illuminated from above. Today the overhead illumination comes from the glass bricks set in the roof by Stuart Piggott in 1956. When the stones were being carved, if the roof was missing, it was the overhead sun that cast shadows while the sculptors worked.

In the south-west chamber at the top of Stone 14 in a line there are three cup-depressions which, although thought not to be artificial, may explain the choice of the stone. Three cups could hint at the presence of the triple goddess because in this chamber Stuart Piggott found that 'three skulls had been arranged against the south wall' in a row: *those of a child, a young woman, and an elderly woman.* These may have served as a practical and visible allusion to the three ages of woman.

In 1859 Dr Thurnam explored the end-chamber at the west and a part of the central passage. Besides the human skeletons a roebuck antler was found, and 10cm (4 ins) from it lay a rib between two ball-like sarsen nodules. The purpose of these objects may have been to make a 'readable' statement about female and male fertility respectively, and in the funerary context of a barrow this extends to the desire for rebirth.

Along the northern interior of the megalithic barrow, inside the forecourt and inside the gallery, there is an amazing sequence of at least five sarsens, all of which seem to carry the impression of heads in left-profile. Starting with and including the ewe's head on Stone 25 and moving outwards, we come to Gallery Stones 31, 35, and 36, and north-side blocking stone 46, all with human heads. There is a sixth head on the left edge of the back of Stone 45 which is the central blocking stone, and possibly a seventh on Stone 23 in the west chamber (and Stones 22 and 21 would make nine). Some are easy to see, but others require the illumination to be just right. It is my belief, however, that the north-side stones would show at their best when they receive the light of the equinoctial rising sun.

All these heads are in left profile which on the gender-handedness theory implies femininity. More may be found—their detection depends sensitively on the conditions and direction of oblique lighting—and some, including right-hand ones, have been seen or suspected on parts of the outside façade and south-side forecourt. For instance, there is Stone 44 mentioned by Michael Dames as being a goddess stone, which has a left eye socket.

A most remarkable carving at this long barrow is among the megaliths introduced as 'blocking stones' when the entrance was sealed. Like the monument which is aligned equinoctially, the façade of blocking stones faces east.

The height of the biggest stone (Stone 45) above ground level is 3.60 metres (11 feet 9 inches). The stone weighs around 20 tons. Running down the middle of its eastern face is a vertical mark, long and narrow, hollowed out in vulvar fashion.

The impression is 160cm (5ft 3ins) long and 50cm (20ins) wide at its maximum. Sculptors have confirmed that it was channelled out by axe grinding and repetitive rubbing and pecking with hard-stone tools at what must have been viewed as a sacred part of a sacred stone. The length of the main part of the scored section is 120cm (4 ft). Centrally positioned is a deeper area running down 130 × 50mm (5 × 21ins) long and 130mm (5ins) deep, which corresponds to the vaginal entrance. There is a lesser mark in the clitoral region. Because the worked area is smooth, lichen has had difficulty taking hold during the 42 years since Piggott's excavation, in contrast to undressed areas elsewhere. For some centuries before this the stone lay flat, having fallen forwards, face down.

The image is similar to the 60-cm long vulva at the Table des Marchands, Locmariaquer in Brittany, which has been studied by Marija Gimbutas (1991) and others (Meaden, 1992 and 1997); but the West Kennet vulva is superior in size, quality, and detail. Its east-facing position ensures that on every cloud-free morning of the year the rising sun impregnates the vulva with radiant light and heat. The best time to photograph it is late morning, say 12 to 12.30 British Summer Time or 11–11.30 GMT, before the sun passes off the face of the stone.

The 20-ton megalith at West Kennet Long Barrow with its huge vulva carving. This east-facing stone stands in line with the barrow's central passage and end-chamber, and suggests that the latter was viewed as the Earth Mother's organs of regeneration with expectations of rebirth in the house of the dead.

The rediscovery of this fertility image has considerable consequences for rebirth theories and the spiritual motivation behind the construction of long barrows. This is the fourth megalith with yoni or grooved vulva so far found in the region (the others are Avebury Stone 106 and Outer Stones II and VI), or it is the eighth if Avebury Stones 32, 31, 4, and 8 can be included.

Several archaeologists, from Tony Cyriax (1921) onwards, have expressed the view that long barrows were intended to duplicate as closely as possible the sexual and reproductive organs of woman, hence female deity. The discovery of a central vulva mark, aligned with the symbolic vagina-womb behind, reinforces the imagery. Other chambered long barrows like the Bridestones in Cheshire are being studied for similar images. It is not impossible that a little to the east of the West Kennet barrow, in line with the vulva stone and gallery, a socket in the chalk may be found which formerly held a stone of phallic shape.

12

ANCIENT STONES ON THE HILL

Harestone Circle and Cove

In sight of the Sanctuary and a kilometre and a half (a mile) to the south, is a stone circle with a pyramidal centre-stone carved with triangular faces. I found this circle on 14 December 1996 and have been unable to discover any previous report of it. High on a hill, on the northern hill-ridge of Harestone Down (SU 1139 6644), it stands near a three-stone arrangement which echoes the setting of a Neolithic cove.

The age of these ordered stones—*Harestone Circle and Cove*—is unknown, but they have enough elements of Neolithic symbolism to warrant an archaeological investigation. A little to the north-east at a lower altitude is East Kennet Long Barrow, with sarsens protruding from its south-eastern end, which is even longer than the one at West Kennet although it has never been opened by archaeologists. West Kennet Long Barrow and Silbury Hill are visible to the north-west.

The possible cove has a huge centre-stone, 10 tons in weight, which has toppled over and lies nearly flat, and there are two megaliths associated with it. On the right is a three-ton sarsen, while a second one of similar mass, which one would expect to be on the left, lies out of position, having fallen inwards across the face of the middle stone. If the structure is a cove, the direction is unique for the Avebury region, for it is that of *the midwinter sunset*. This suggests that the site could be part of the sacred-landscape plan

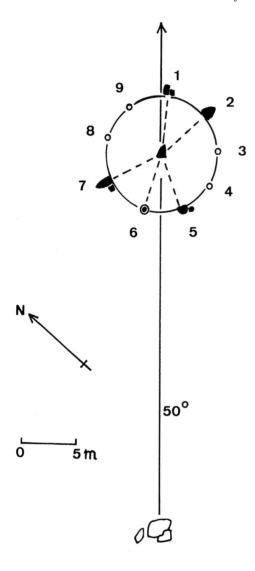

Stone Circle and the presumed Cove on Harestone Down.

At the centre of the 10-metre (33-foot) diameter circle is a quasi-pyramidal standing stone. 1 is a broken sarsen; 2: a fallen triangular sarsen; 5: a fallen sarsen; 6: the stump of a missing sarsen whose bearing from the centre is the Hallowe'en sunset; 7: a splendid high megalith but fallen. Its direction from centre is the May-Festival sunset (62 degrees west of north). 3, 4, 8, 9 are positions suggested for missing stones.

The 'cove' may have faced either midwinter sunset or midsummer sunrise. The bearing from the 'cove' of the centre stone of the circle is 50 degrees east of north. The distance between 'cove' and centre stone is about 35 metres (38 yards).

centred on Avebury. Since Avebury has a cove facing the midsummer sunrise, and Beckhampton a cove to the midwinter sunrise, perhaps two coves were arranged for the solstice sunsets? Might there exist the remains of a midsummer-sunset cove whose location is yet to be uncovered? On the other hand, it is possible that the cove at Harestone— if it really is one—faced the opposite way, the direction of midsummer sunrise, because its bearing to the centre of the stone circle is that of the midsummer sunrise.

Viewed from what I suggest is a cove, the pyramidal stone stands at the centre of the circle 35 metres (38 yards) away, boldly upright against the sky. Its circle 10 metres

(33 feet) in diameter has four surviving perimeter stones as well as the stump of a fifth. The biggest is about eight tons. All four have fallen, and one has broken into three pieces of which two remain. Another has broken off at the base—the bottom part in position, the top lying outwards. The third stone, another triangular stone at the east side of the circle, has also fallen outwards. The fourth stone, also complete, is a tall, robust megalith lying to the west-south-west. Even with its base in the air it impresses because of its hugeness.

These lichen-covered megaliths are set deeply in the earth. They could be of Neolithic or Bronze Age date. As Michael Pitts commented when he saw them on 28 May, 1997: 'Only excavation can tell. This is certainly not a natural disposition of stones. It would make a good exercise for the television Time Team.'

The inclusion of sarsens with pyramidal or triangular symmetry smacks of Neolithic/Bronze Age feminine symbolism which appears again and again in the Avebury region. Because of the central pyramidal stone, it seems unlikely that the stones are the remains of an unrecognised barrow. They are best viewed in the winter when the grass is short.

Can this be another ritual centre, a southerly outpost of the vast Neolithic landscape of which Avebury constitutes the low-lying centre and Windmill Hill the northern heights? Or are the stones prehistoric ones, but rearranged and re-used by a later

Harestone Down, near East Kennet Long Barrow. On the hill-crest is a circle of fallen stones with a standing pyramidal stone at its centre. A short distance away are three disturbed stones which may constitute a cove.

people? Whatever the answer, because of its considerable altitude, the site would be well placed for the lighting of beacons.

Despite the smallness of the circle's diameter, two stones may have been orientated to indicate the February/Imbolc and May Day sunsets—which means the Early August and Hallowe'en sunsets too; in other words, the chief fire festivals are represented, approximately, by the two stones. We know from Celtic traditions one reason for fire-lighting ceremonies in later times: the intention was to 'rekindle' the sun at the start of the Celtic New Year which was early November or Hallowe'en/Samhain. The duration of the Celtic Early-August festival was the longest of the year. In Ireland it became the tradition for the ever-lengthening festival Lughnasad to last from mid-July to mid-August. The name for the Irish Lugh, who was a powerful deity, is related to the Latin *lux* (light) or *lucus* (grove)—and is descended from words related to the Sumerian *lug*, meaning sun.

There are plenty of sarsens on this hill-ridge, but many are so disturbed as to make any reconstruction of their original arrangements questionable; however, some at least appear to have been deeply earthfast for centuries if not millennia, and many are

A megalith close to Harestone Stone Circle displaying yonic symbolism typical of the British Neolithic. This is a fine deeply grooved stone, to which class Station Stone 91 at Stonehenge belongs.

Langdean Stone Circle as it is today. Only one stone has been displaced since A. D. Passmore drew his plan in 1926 and that was external to the main circular setting.

indicated on the 2500:1 Ordnance Survey map of 1883. Sherds of Early Bronze Age pottery have been recovered from two deposits within 100 metres (110 yards) of the hill-ridge.

Only a little distance to the south-west of the stone circle there is a fine stone with a deep vertical groove. If this is Neolithic symbolic imagery, then a megalith sacred to the local Earth Goddess may have been intended. More than with any other surviving megalith in the Avebury region, the name Kauri-stone could apply to this stone, because the groove resembles the slit of the cowrie-shell which has been the universal divine yoni from extremely ancient to modern times. In Hindu religious lore the megalith would be treated as a stone manifestation of the Goddess Devi-Kunti, and the cowrie-shell was her talisman.

Although the site can be reached along a public right of way the stones are on private land, a distant part of the Family Read's farm of Stanton Saint Bernard.

Eight hundred metres (875 yards) to the south-east, in a valley bottom and again on private land (tenanted by Roger Harley of East Kennet Farm), is *Langdean Stone Circle*, first described by A. D. Passmore in 1926 (SU 1177 6574). It is about 5 to 6 metres (16 to 20 feet) in diameter and has a twin-stone entrance at the west. East of the centre is an offset standing stone, a thin slab one metre (3 feet) high. The sarsen stones could be from the Neolithic/Bronze Age because of the shapes and positions of some of them. Close by, to the south-west, is a fine lozenge-type megalith two metres (6 feet) long, fallen and partly covered with turf.

This stone circle examined by Passmore in 1921 may prove to be a foundation ring for supporting the floor of a hut, of remote but unknown age. One big megalith, beyond the circle's perimeter, has been displaced since Passmore's time. A recent description has been given by Neil Mortimer (1997). Not far to the east (SU 1185 6519) are two rows of low-set sarsen stones about 10 metres (11 yards) apart and 40 metres (44 yards) long. They make up a long rectangle, running roughly west-east, with three transverse rows. The enclosed area is a little lower than outside, and the possibility of a prehistoric building or long house was suggested by Leslie Grinsell (1957) rather than a stone avenue as proposed by others.

13

NEOLITHIC RUINS AND MYSTERIES

Megalithic monuments north of Avebury

There is a wealth of megalithic monuments all round Avebury. Let's look now at those to the north, starting from the most northerly source of the streams that feed the Kennet.

First is the Neolithic or Bronze Age stone circle near the village of *Winterbourne Bassett*. The remains of this double concentric circle, with diameters about 70 and 45–50 metres (75 and 50–55 yards), lie six kilometres (4 miles) north of Avebury and four kilometres (2½ miles) north of Windmill Hill. The circle may have been important in its prime because the apparent complexity and huge size suggest that it was a place of high ceremony used by a large community.

Little is left of this ruined site (SU 094 755) whose fallen stones lie in a tree-lined field on the north side of the road. William Stukeley wrote in 1743: 'At Winterburn-basset, a little north of Abury, in a field north-west of the church, upon elevated ground, is a double circle of stones concentric, 60 cubits diameter. The two circles are near one another, so that one may walk between. Many of the stones have of late been carry'd away. West of it is a single, broad, flat, and high stone, standing by itself.' (Stukeley's indication of 60 cubits for the diameter is wrong, as this would imply 33 metres (36 yards). He probably meant radius as John Barnatt has pointed out. Stukeley's little-known sketch of these circles is held in the Bodleian Library, Oxford (as Gough Maps 231, fol.216).

Fewer than ten inconspicuous stones survive, and as some are rather flat and all have fallen, it is best to inspect them when the grass is short. Geophysical surveying, and later excavation, should one day locate the positions of missing stones as empty stone-holes in the chalk. The flat-faced, broad, standing stone on the south-west edge of the opposite side of the road is modern, erected only a few years ago.

The winter springs which erupt from the downs hereabouts join to form the source of the Winterbourne stream. One brook passes just to the north of the stone circles. Before reaching Avebury the Winterbourne flows through *Winterbourne Monkton* where the church has a 12th-century font with a naked fertility goddess engraved on one side. What is more, the lady vaunts a big belly and open vulva from which emerges

This 12th-century stone font with a fertility goddess engraved on it can be seen in the church at Winterbourne Monkton north of Avebury. Outside, one can see a multi-pitted sarsen from Millbarrow which has been re-used as a gravestone.

William Stukeley's drawing of Millbarrow as it was in 1723. One of the megaliths was taken
to the nearby churchyard where it continues in service as a gravestone.

spring vegetation. This would seem to be the Earth Goddess giving seasonal birth to
abundant plantlife. A sickle held in one hand touches a zig-zag band of chevrons which
experts in primitive symbolic art interpret as water signs. Above is the coil of a left-
handed spiral. The composition suggests that the early Church had to contend here
with the country folk's desires for a limited degree of continuing reverence for the traditional fertility goddess. It was taking a long time to suppress the old rustic habits.

Four hundred metres (440 yards) west of Monkton there was once a splendid chambered long barrow—sketched by John Aubrey and William Stukeley—known as
Millbarrow, of which limited parts survived, despite heavy damage, until 1967 when
a new landowner chose to 'improve' the area, concreted the track, and removed the
little that was left of mound and sarsens (SU 0943 7220). The site had never been
fully scheduled as an ancient monument, although its progressive deterioration was

William Stukeley's drawing of Shelving Stone which used to be less than a mile north of
Avebury but has since been demolished.

occasionally commented upon by antiquarians. C. T. Barker (1984) summarises the
depressing tale and Alasdair Whittle's excellent report on his excavation of surviving
subsurface features was published in 1994. In John Aubrey's drawing a long barrow
with rectangular stone chamber at its east is shown bordered by 29 small upright
sarsens.

At least one megalith from Millbarrow survives. It lies in the churchyard where,
according to a church pamphlet, it marks the grave of Reverend Brinsden who died
in 1710. The stone is 2.5 metres (8 feet) long, heavily pitted all over, and weighs about
3 tons. Other Millbarrow megaliths are suspected of being in the walls of neighbouring houses, gardens and farms.

Two kilometres (1¼ miles) east of Monkton, under the Hackpen escarpment, is a
long mound from which a few small sarsens protrude (SU 1163 7230). When John
Merewether looked at it 150 years ago he described a façade of eight megaliths at its
south-western end.

South-east of Monkton is the site of *Shelving Stone* (SU 1037 7156), the nearest
chambered barrow to Avebury and 1,300 metres (1,400 yards) north of the henge. It
was already badly damaged when Aubrey and Stukeley saw and sketched it. The capstone of a collapsed megalithic chamber then lay at an angle upon two side stones,
but the whole had been demolished by 1849. The capstone's dimensions, 8ft by 5ft
by one foot, suggest a weight of only about 4 tons.

A kilometre (½ mile) to the east of this site is a stone circle 6 metres (20 feet) in diameter made of megaliths weighing up to 3 tons each (SU 1142 7126). At first glance the site could well be named *Avebury Down Stone Circle*, because that is what we see today on Avebury Down, but it would be more correct to call it a bell barrow. Old Ordnance Survey maps mark it as a stone circle; recent ones state 'tumulus'. O. G. S. Crawford inspected it in 1921 and prepared a plan. In 1998 there were still seven megaliths, as well as scattered fragments of others, the same as in 1921. One of the fragments has fallen over, and at its centre can be seen the mark made by the iron wedge used to break it. Two of the biggest megaliths (Stones 1 and 7) stand in their original positions. The fallen Stone 5 has a lozenge shape. Stone 6 is heavily pitted with tiny holes of the type often selected by Stone-Age/Bronze builders (like the Millbarrow stone).

When John Merewether inspected the Avebury Down circle in 1849, there were eight megaliths together with four sockets from which other stones had recently been removed. From inside the circle Merewether unearthed some rude pottery, bones of animals, bits of charcoal, and the teeth of deer, oxen and swine. This suggests it was devised as a stone ring which came to contain one or more pits holding offerings. Crawford says that 'in the centre are traces of a central stone no longer visible', but these could be the traces of Merewether's activity. The site would be worth excavating properly. Three kilometres (2 miles) to the west the equinoctial sun sets over Windmill Hill and two kilometres (1¼ miles) to the south-west is Avebury Henge, the direction of extreme southerly moonset. O. G. S. Crawford noted that the site was 2,400 feet (740 metres) due south of a large upright sarsen, but this has since disappeared. A. D. Passmore, writing of this little circle in 1926, said that together with the Langdean Circle and one other which formerly existed at Monkton, they 'form a small group of a class that are common in Scotland but rare in this part of England.'

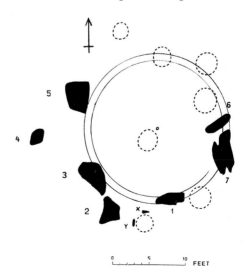

Plan of the stone circle on Avebury Down drawn in 1922 by O. G. S. Crawford who called it the Pennings Circle. Stones 1 and 7 are standing; the others have fallen. Broken circles indicate depressions in the turf where fallen or upright stones may have been. The only change since 1922 is that the fragment marked X has fallen sideways. The big circles indicate the possible course followed by the original stones. The site is now called Pennings Bell Barrow.

Avebury Down: Circle of megaliths recently scheduled as Pennings Bell Barrow,
two kilometres north-east of the henge.

The site is on gently sloping ground with traces of a circular platform and slight
mound about 16 metres (50 feet) in diameter, beyond which is a 3-metre (10-foot)
strip of land and then a perimeter ditch now filled in. In the *Victoria County History
of Wiltshire*, Leslie Grinsell suggests that the site is a bowl barrow (number 49a)
bordered by a ring of stones, but it seems more likely that it was built either as a bell
barrow with an internal ring of 12 large megaliths, or as a stone circle converted into
a species of bell barrow. No burial has been found, however, and the sarsens are abnor-
mally big for the perimeter stone ring (peristalith) of a small barrow. In contrast, close
by there are several well preserved conventional bowl barrows of great height and
diameter.

Whatever this unusual site actually is, it looks like a ring of stones dating from the
Neolithic or Bronze Age and is well worth a visit. The site is best approached from
Avebury, starting west up the hill to the downs (along Green Street) before turning
north at SU 1137 7044 where a direct track to Hackpen Hill is signposted.

14

SACRED RIVER GODDESS

Megalithic monuments south of Avebury

The waters sacred to the people of Avebury run on to the village and then to Silbury, east of which, on the river bed, lies a band of sarsen stones (SU 1029 6872). They may have begun as stepping stones (the Silbury Steps), but it is not known whether any were used in ancient times.

Half-a-kilometre (¼ mile) farther on *Swallowhead Spring* erupts (SU 1010 6806). It is here that the river changes its name to Kennet—until the eighteenth century pronounced Cunnit. Nearly 2,000 years ago the Roman town Cunetio at Marlborough was named after the river. This is another river-name which may hark back to the time of a long-forgotten river goddess (as with the Severn (Celtic Sabraan, Roman Sabrina), Seine (Gaulish Sequana), Ganges (Hindu Ganga, still a much-revered goddess) and thousands of others). There is another River Cunnit, modernised to Kennet, in Suffolk, and a River Kunnit in Kerala in southern India where the Goddess Kunda or Kunti lives on as a well-loved deity.

Swallowhead is phonetically similar to Suilohead and may come from the same root as the Goddess name Sul (as is true of the Celtic Goddess Sul at nearby Bath, who is considered to be equivalent to the Goddess Brigit under another name), so this may be a lost name for the Goddess of Silbury Hill.

Lawrence Durdin-Robertson refers to a suggestion by Morgan who points out that Sul derives from the Celtic for 'eye' (*suil*) and 'seeing' and might therefore be connected to the Silbury Goddess. The winter waters of the sacred Suilohead Spring provided the sacred link with Silbury which in wet winters is encircled with water. The Suilo Spring is then said to be flowing because 'the Goddess Sul or Suil has come to the mound and fed the spring'.

Rachel Pollack (1997) cites R. J. Stewart who says that Old Irish *sul* or *suil* meant not only eye and cavity but also vulva/vagina—which again leads to Suilo-spring (Swallowspring, Swallowhead) and Silbury.

In 1858 William Long told of a traditional culinary custom still being observed at Swallowhead. Sugar was mixed with water from the fertile spring and eaten with cakes and figs (the latter regarded as a feminine fertility fruit *par excellence* because of its vulva-shape when opened and its plentiful seeds). Avebury villagers then went in procession to the top of Silbury on Palm Sunday to complete the tradition, maintaining an ancient fertility rite which was permitted because it was probably not fully understood by the Church.

William Stukeley had reported the same practice in his Avebury book over a century earlier (1743: 43–44): 'The country people have an anniversary meeting at the top of Silbury-hill on every Palm-sunday, when they make merry with cakes, figs, sugar, and water fetch'd from the Swallow-head, or spring of the Kennet. This Spring was much more remarkable than at present, gushing out of the earth, in a continued stream. They say it was spoil'd by digging for a fox who earth'd above, in some cranny thereabouts; this disturb'd the sacred nymphs, in a poetical way of speaking.'

Palm Sunday is the Sunday in March or April which precedes Easter Sunday. This suggests that in pagan times the tradition had been a spring equinox celebration, the people rejoicing that winter was behind them and the rites of spring were beginning. Instead of ending the custom against the people's will, the Church switched the date, to make the locals forget its original purpose. Rites-of-spring traditions in one form or another could date from the Silbury era, or even from the earliest West Kennet long barrow period when the internal spring murals were being carved.

A kilometre (1,100 yards) south of Silbury is a sarsen site, now empty, on higher land towards Allington Down, which is called *Beckhampton Penning* or sometimes 'Avebury South', being in the parish of Avebury although three kilometres (2 miles) from the henge. The site (at SU 0985 6714) was made up of many sarsens at one time, but its shape and purpose remain unclear. Stukeley (1743: 46) named it South Downs Barrow: 'Upon this heath south of Silbury-hill was a very large oblong work, like a long barrow, made only of stones pitch'd in the ground, no tumulus. Mr Smith beforemention'd told me his cousin took away the stones (then) 14 years ago, to make mere stones withal. I take it to have been an archdruid's, tho' humble, yet magnificent; being 350 feet or 200 cubits long.'

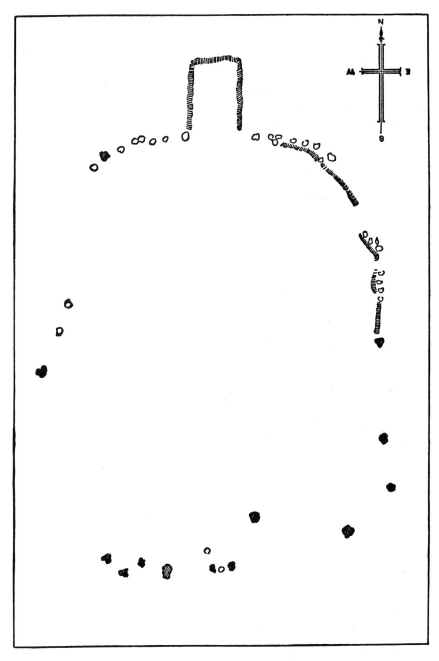

The setting of sarsen stones at Beckhampton Penning, a little over a kilometre south of Silbury Hill as recorded by A. C. Smith. The length was about 80 metres (88 yards) and the width 66 metres (72 yards).

In Alfred Charles Smith's time (1885) 22 small sarsens were still there, set in a rough oval measuring about 80 by 66 metres (88 by 72 yards). Some people thought this to be another of the region's stone 'circles'.

Leslie Grinsell (1957) reported that by 1950 the stones were 'lying in heaps and probably hardly any in situ'. Their complete absence today shows that farmers, when left to themselves, continue shifting prehistoric stones which should be wholly protected. Good accounts of this monument have been given by C. T. Barker (1984) and Neil Mortimer (1998).

The Kennet flows on, to be joined by the intermittent waters of Waden Spring, and immediately passes east-west through the middle of a double-ringed *Late Neolithic palisaded enclosure* (SU 112 682) at *West Kennet*, which has been excavated in recent years by Alasdair Whittle. The rings consisted of closely set oak posts up to 40 cm (16 ins) thick which may have been 6 metres (20 feet) high in the outer circle and 8 metres (26 feet) high in the inner circle. The maximum diameters of these circles were 230 and 180 metres (250 and 200 yards), which led Alasdair Whittle to suggest that they were sacred precincts in the style of neighbouring Late Neolithic sites. A second timber structure once stood alongside the first, 336 metres (367 yards) at its maximum diameter but more oval in outline, its longest axis directed towards Silbury Hill. Dr Whittle expresses the view that such precincts or 'holy rings' (the words used in the title of his book published in 1997) 'were perhaps part of the process of labour mobilisation for the monumental undertaking of the mound'. Silbury he also discussed as a 'sacred mound', and he reviewed analogies from other cultures, including the Mississipian culture of North America. In discussing the palisade monuments and Silbury Hill, Dr Whittle appears to favour the view that the motive for building such labour-intensive monuments can arise for religious reasons, in this case monuments which use a sacred river in a traditional sacred landscape, and with ancestral West Kennet Long Barrow looming to the south. Silbury 'might have stood as a metaphor of the earth, and as a symbol of renewal' (1997) which, to use archaic religious terminology, means a female earth deity and a cyclic view of time.

A little farther on the river passes within 350 metres (380 yards) of the Sanctuary to its north and *Langdean* and *Harestone Circles* between one and two kilometres (½ and 1¼ miles) to the south, as we saw in chapter 12. Three hundred metres (330 yards) north of the Sanctuary and just west of the *Ridgeway* as indicated on the 1925 map, were *Circles of Stones* at SU 1186 6835 and 1187 6836. By the early 1950s no traces above ground remained. Leslie Grinsell (1957) thought the Ordnance Surveyors had seen two adjacent round barrows with a sarsen kerb-ring.

Also, somewhere to their north, on the 'hills between West Kennet and Avebury', were *two concentric stone circles* set around a burial mound which was opened and destroyed about 1882, as reported in *Wiltshire Archaeological Magazine*, volume 20. There was a central pile or cairn of sarsens (originally soil-covered) about seven metres

(23 feet) in diameter, and two metres (six feet) from its edge were the concentric rings of big sarsen stones, some weighing several tons. A crouched skeleton lay in a central grave which was partly lined with sarsens and covered with flat stones at ground level.

A few kilometres farther east and the waters pass a lost stone circle site at Clatford, called *the Broadstones*. John Aubrey reported it first: 'In a Lane from Kynet towards Marleborough, doe lie fall'n down, eight huge stones in a Circle.'

In his *Itinerarium Curiosum* (1724, Part 1: 132) and field notes William Stukeley said that the circle was 'over against Clatford at a flexure in the river', that the biggest stone measured 16½ × 6 ft (5 metres by 2 metres), and that four neighbouring stones 'may possibly have been the beginning of an Avenue'. All the stones were stolen in the late nineteenth century. O. Meyrick in 1955 calculated that the site was at SU 163 689 at the 'flexure' 100 metres (110 yards) west of Plough Cottage near the road, where the river makes almost a right-angled turn. The name of this narrow field,

General view, looking south-east, of Devil's Den in Clatford Bottom, whose great capstone has heads on it, three facing left, one facing right.

recorded as Bradstonemede or similar, can be traced back to 1466. Only 200 metres (220 yards) to the north-east one of the richest-known female burials beneath a round barrow has been discovered, a position which Meyrick thought was significantly close to the stone circle and to the river.

Eight hundred metres (880 yards) to the north, along the Clatford Valley, is the Neolithic structure known as *Devil's Den* (SU 1520 6965). In his Avebury book William Stukeley published three sketches of this monument. A huge capstone is supported by three main megaliths, two of them collapsed; but their security has been assured by a concreting operation directed by Passmore in 1921.

In the Neolithic era, mounting the 20-ton capstone above the others would have posed a tremendous challenge. The vertical megaliths must have been set up firmly first, and then, quite possibly, a mound was raised outside and between them. A very long ramp could have been built next, along which the capstone was dragged until it lay on top of the vertical monoliths, after which both mound and ramp would be removed as far as possible. Such an operation, if correct, would explain why the stones of Devil's Den now stand on an obviously artificial eminence; and why the much-spread remains of a long mound orientated NW-SE, about 70 metres (230 feet) long and 40 metres (130 feet) broad, were seen and described by Passmore in 1922. One should not necessarily assume that the stones are the remains of a chambered long barrow, although they might be (in which case the ramp would have remained to serve as the long mound). Flanking ditches, like those at West and East Kennet, have not been found, but this is not an essential criterion. The stones could have been raised to form a dolmen in the fashion more typical of western areas, in which case it might share the spiritual characteristics expected of a cove. Whether barrow or dolmen, the construction is perhaps directed at the early November sunrise, or, if it is a dolmen, towards the May Eve sunset as Norman Lockyer was the first to observe (1909).

In fact, there is another good reason to suppose that the monument might have been a dolmen-type structure: its capstone seems to have profiles of heads carved upon two, perhaps three, of its sides, suggesting that, if the art was meant to be seen, the capstone was never covered with earth.

In all there could be two or three left-profile human heads and one right-profile head. Looking from the south-east, the top left corner shows a strong head in left-profile facing south-west. Then, moving clockwise, just on the other side of the same edge is an ugly, possibly reptilian, head in right profile looking south-eastwards. Continuing on, what may or may not be a head faces about 290 degrees, and another possible left-facing head gazes to the south-east. Further visits under differing light conditions are needed to clarify these observations. Photographs of two of the heads, each with eye, nose and mouth, are included here. If this can be classed as a female-deity structure like West Kennet Long Barrow, the name Devi's Den would be appropriate.

Although a public right of way passes close to the monument, the structure itself is

Two of the heads on the capstone of Devil's Den.

on private arable land owned by Mr Routh of Clatford, from whom permission for access should be sought.

From Clatford the river flows to Marlborough, passing close to the 20-metre (66-foot) high Marlborough Mount which may correspond to Silbury, and then to Cunetio—the Roman town named after the river almost 2,000 years ago. Kintbury too, in Berkshire, derives its name from the river which at Reading flows into the Thames (itself named after a river goddess).

15

ARTEFACTS AND SYMBOLISM

Worked objects of Neolithic origin, apparently non-utilitarian, have been found at several sites in the Avebury region. They are interesting because they help us to understand as far as we can what symbols and images meant to the Neolithic people.

During the excavations of the 1930s on Windmill Hill, fragile chalk carvings were found which can only survive when they are sheltered by the infill of pits and ditches (Smith 1965: 130–5). These include two phalluses, 90 and 80mm (3½ and 3ins) long, which were thought to be male fertility objects, and 30 chalk balls, the biggest 74mm (3ins) in diameter and the smallest 37mm (1½ins). Fourteen balls have diameters in the range 50–60mm (2–2½ins). Most are carved from gritty chalk containing fossil shell fragments, and the surfaces of two were decorated with tiny dot-sized pits. The excavators mentioned specifically that sixteen of the 30 were found in pairs.

Another type of carving is represented by objects carved with cups, grooves or complete perforations. In all, eight chalk pieces each had a cup hollowed into one side. The cups are either round hollows occupying a central position or oblong hollows scraped on a smoothed surface of otherwise irregular lumps. Isobel Smith offers a possible interpretation by saying that these artificial cup-marks may 'express an idea symbolised elsewhere by cup-marks worked in stone' and that this agrees with observations made by Nicholas Thomas in 1952. The latter sees them—here and elsewhere, as at Wilsford and Woodhenge for instance—as ritual objects with vulvar fertility implications. Isobel Smith adds that the depressions hollowed into the side of one of the phalluses may be interpreted this way too.

There are also large and small chunks of chalk perforated by drilling conical pits from opposite sides. Sometimes the penetration is perfect, sometimes misaligned. Several have straight or curving grooved lines scored on them as well. One is a small fossil sponge with a natural pit in the middle of one face, centred upon which are two straight lines hand-cut at right angles, the whole surrounded by an incised circle (Smith 1965: Fig. 57).

Two chalk objects from Windmill Hill were classified by the excavators as crudely shaped shouldered figurines representing headless and armless human figures. The division between the thighs is defined by a deep vertical groove.

Another fascinating object from this site is a carved chalk lozenge—originally 120 mm (4¼ins) in length—with grooves and a central hole, which I described in chapter 1. Elsewhere, around a dozen flints knapped into lozenges were found at a single site in the Avebury district, suggesting application as votives, charms or talismans. One lozenge, not made of flint, bears a central groove carved in the middle where the Windmill Hill chalk lozenge had its hole pierced.

Fossiliferous oolitic lozenge with bored central cup 5mm (¼in) in diameter. Length 230mm (9ins), weight 1.1kg (2lb 6oz), 25 January 1997.

I picked up a similar cup-centred lozenge, made of limestone oolite, at West Kennet on 25 January, 1997. Its longest diagonal is 165mm (6½ins), the shortest 140mm (5½ ins) and it weighs 1080g (38oz). In this region loose surface finds of pre-Iron Age minerals are usually of flint and sarsen, and only rarely some other stone. The precise spot where I found it was the west-to-east public footpath that links the north-to-south barrow footpath to Gunsight Lane (SU 1070 6816).

It lay with broken flints and small irregular chunks of sarsen on the soil surface, its upper side cleaned by rain, the underside dirt-filled, and at its centre there was a drilled, round depression like a cup or pit 5mm (¼in) in diameter within a bigger dished area 15mm (½in) in diameter. Despite its crudeness and the damage suffered from plough and weather, there is enough to suggest that this oolitic lozenge may be a mystical cult-object or charm from an age of fertility worship.

Oolite is a fossil-filled rock brought to West Kennet and other localities in the Neolithic Age for use in dry-stone walls, filling gaps between the orthostats of the sarsen chambers of the barrow. Its origin is outcrops or quarries in the Bath-Wellow region of the Southern Cotswolds 30 kilometres (18 miles) to the west. The long bar-row at Stoney Littleton near Wellow is made entirely of this type of stone.

The stone lozenge may have arrived with a load of other oolite stones. The chance lozenge shape was noted and some devotee, aware of its fertility significance, added the central dot by rotating the tip of a harder stone against it. Limestone does not nat-urally fracture into polygons, rhombs or quasi-lozenges as sarsen does, so it seems likely that the shape was accidental or deliberate. The stone could have travelled down the sloping field over the centuries from a deposit higher up, such as a shrine, burial cist or round barrow. Carved lozenges with central cup-marks dating from the British Neolithic and Bronze Ages have been found elsewhere too.

Near the same public footpath fifteen months earlier (14 October, 1995, at SU 1068 6816) I found a 170-mm (6½-in) long flint 'phallus'; 30–40mm (1¼–1½ins) thick and with a smooth rounded end, its appearance as a realistic penis had been improved by striking four or five careful blows along its length to achieve the desired shape.

From a primary level in one of Windmill Hill's ditches has come the spiral shell of a large whelk. The apex is broken off and there is a small rectangular hole in the side. Isobel Smith commented that the shell did not appear to have been fresh when chanced upon by the Neolithic collector (that is, it was not gathered as food but was saved for symbolic or sentimental reasons). Another ditch produced the conical-triangular shell of a limpet from a Late Neolithic level.

From the secondary filling of the long barrow at West Kennet Stuart Piggott unearthed some 20 beads of bone, stone (shale, lignite or jet) and shells (Piggott 1962: 51–53). The latter were six seashells which had been perforated as if to thread them on a cord or string. They included two cowries (*Cypraea*) and three spiral shells. One, a perforated dog-whelk, is similar to one from the Nympsfield barrow at Coaley Peak

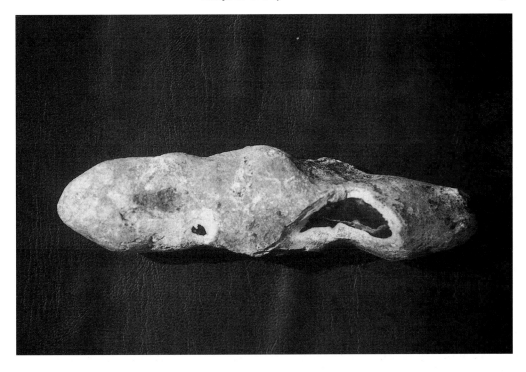

A probable flint phallus 170mm (6½ins) long, found at West Kennet in October 1995.

in the Cotswolds. Stuart Piggott notes that cowries from British waters were widely used as beads, and cites instances from Langton (East Yorkshire) and a barrow near Dorchester in addition to the north-east and south-east chambers at West Kennet Long Barrow.

The finest of the pots from the latter barrow is the much-photographed Bell Beaker from the secondary filling, which had been placed not far beneath the capstone of the north-west chamber. It is beautifully and heavily decorated with a repetitive lozenge pattern and chevron band of a type found fairly widely on the Continent.

In the *Wiltshire Archaeological Magazine* in 1955 Nicholas Thomas discussed the contents of a Neolithic pit which had been found 42 years earlier on the top of Waden Hill (Stukeley wrote Weedon-hill). The pit was 108 metres (118 yards) north and east of a pond (now a covered reservoir) near the crest of the hill. Besides many sherds of plain Windmill Hill ware, animal bones, and flint tools which lay in a black earthy material, there was a sarsen hammerstone. Its edges were roughened with use, one face retaining 'the smooth red surface typical of some weathered sarsen'. Nicholas Thomas concluded there was probably an early Neolithic habitation site on Waden Hill, and this was supported by remarks made by W. E. V. Young, the Avebury

One of four left-facing heads from Waden Hill.

Museum curator, that depressions on the ground had led him to suspect a prehistoric habitation on the top too.

Knowing nothing of this, I was attracted to the top of Waden Hill by a map-reading prediction based on the hill-top intersection of a well-defined midsummer-sunrise sight-line with a huge lynchet which rises in a south-westerly direction from near Stone 37 of the Kennet Avenue. The lynchet indicates a long-used and therefore ancient field boundary, so I was looking for a prehistoric path leading towards Silbury Hill, with the possibility of spotting surface signs of human activity at the hill-crest. At this time (April 1997) a new fence had just been installed along the field edge, and stones which the post-hole makers encountered at the hill-crest had been pushed aside. Here (SU 1061 6891) I found two small sarsens, recently unearthed, which bore crude indications of human heads.

One was a 48-kg (106-lb) block with evidence of tooled left and right-side features among the natural lumps and bumps (reference number H8). The other sarsen (H9),

A pair of sarsens found together at the top of Waden Hill. Similar pairings of left-facing heads with stones indicative of female pubic triangles have been found on four occasions so far in the region. Goddess symbolism at ancient shrines is inferred in order to account for this.

weighing 9kg (20lb) had an almost flat-sided head in left-facing profile. There was some evidence of ancient tooling.

Over the next 10 metres (11 yards), with the top of Silbury Hill just in sight, there were half-a-dozen more disturbed sarsens, one a triangular-shaped stone (reference PT 6, weight 15kg (33lb) and two which suggested left-profile heads (H10, weight 9kg (20lb) and H18, weight estimated at 60kg (132lb).

A sarsen head from the river Kennet photographed in situ, 10 February, 1997. This simple piece, 250mm (10ins) long, weight 925 grammes (2lb) has left eye, nose and nostrils, the eye and nostrils pierced through.

The four sarsens with possible heads show them in left-side profile besides which one has a right-side profile too. Could this place have been a shrine, perhaps involving the midsummer sunrise by virtue of the alignment?

A few days earlier (31 March, 1997) I had found another left-profile head (H6) at a field corner (SU 1093 6892) almost due east of the Waden hill-top site. This 70-kg (154-lb) head was in the middle of the Kennet Avenue valley and lay with other sarsens in a small dump resulting from field clearance, so its original position is unknown. The same comment applies to the 12-kg (26-lb) sarsen with a possible left-side head (H11) found at SU 1040 6815 close to the River Kennet and 300 metres (330 yards) from Swallowhead. Part of the 'head' seems to have been dressed. This makes six possible sarsen heads, all in left profile, but with one having a right profile too.

Besides these, I have found three sarsen 'heads' when inspecting the dry bed of the River Kennet. The best (H4) was found on 10 February, 1997 in the West Kennet section (at SU 1126 6818). This small human head weighs 925g (2lb) and has a most delicate outline which includes an eye pierced through the stone and two nostrils joined by a narrow passage! Either this is a quite remarkable, wholly natural piece or it has been partly shaped by hand.

The bed of the Kennet is likely to yield many secrets but the major finds will lie deep in the silt and should be left undisturbed for the archaeologists of the future.

16

SACRED MARRIAGE AT STONEHENGE

Since *Stonehenge* is so near to Avebury, built as a neighbouring monument and contemporary with Avebury in its greatest epoch, I wondered whether similar sculptures were created there also. For a long period there would have been close co-operation between the Avebury and Stonehenge peoples, especially while megaliths were being selected, shaped and transported from the Avebury Hills to Stonehenge. Similarities of religious ritual and philosophy would not be unexpected, leading to affinities of design and execution; and this appears to have happened. One major discovery at Stonehenge involves religious cosmic imagery at the solstices; another provides choice human-head carvings, which I detected after a fresh (and ongoing) appraisal of the stones.

The most obvious head at Stonehenge is a magnificent relief carving which I noticed in 1996 on the vertical western edge of Trilithon 54.

The features are carved to a depth of 50 to 80mm, or two to three inches. The prominent eyebrows, nose and mouth show up clearly, *but only for less than an hour each day* when the sun is shining between 1.50 and 2.40 p.m. in the period from March to October. This is equivalent to 12.50 to 1.40 GMT wintertime, but in the winter the low rays of the sun fail to illuminate the lines of the upper lips. This restricts the period of observation of what is a poorer image to 1.00 to 1.30 GMT, or even less, in the midwinter months.

The carved head on Stone 54 at Stonehenge.
25 August, 3.25 p.m. BST, 2.25 p.m. GMT.

The distinguished face is at its best under a high-altitude summer sun which suggests that its purpose was related to the summer, perhaps a midday event at a summer festival, but certainly not to any winter occasion.

These limitations as to time of day, the unequivocal need for sunshine, and the ever-deepening thickness of lichen, all help to explain why for so many centuries this perfectly executed carving has gone unnoticed. Yet in the summer when the sun is shining it is so easy to see, even from the public footpath at a distance of 15 to 50 metres (50 to 160 feet).

Next there is the Heel Stone, that great megalith placed apart from the other stones beyond the circular earthwork in the direction of midsummer sunrise. It has up to three heads in left profile, while at the north-west a side-view in right, presumably male, profile appears to be at its best on midsummer morning.

I have previously discussed the fairly obvious south-facing head on the Heel Stone in *Stonehenge: The Secret of the Solstice* (p. 130). This head does not face the monument to its south-west; it looks past it southwards. This well-known 'face' seems not entirely accidental: the monument users may have noted a chance facial resemblance in the stone and then made a slight improvement to some particular feature, for example to the left eye. The corresponding right side can also be recognised as a face.

The second head on the Heel Stone can be seen in left profile along the north-west side of the stone and also in right profile when viewing from the roadside. There may also be a small left-profile head close to the top of the stone. The right-profile head is most striking when viewed from the north-east under the light of the midsummer rising sun. This is the only time of year when *sunrise rays* can reach it. Perhaps the people thought this strengthened the stone's male component just as the sunlight reaching the Altar or Goddess Stone activated the monument's female component. The prominent right eye, nose and chin show up well for several minutes during which obliging shadows edge slowly across the side of the face.

It is appropriate that this male head was positioned to serve the Stonehenge monument at this time of the day, appearing at its best at the moment when the Heel Stone assumes the role of 'Fal' in the sunrise Midsummer Marriage with the Earth Mother. The presence of this head on the megalith is surely no accident: even a limited amount of pecking with hardstone tools must have been necessary.

There are indications of heads on other stones, too. The one on Stone 53 has a straight nose almost as long as the sculptured nose on Stone 54. The nose seems to have been made in the direction of pre-existing holes that were treated as eyes. The head faces south and is best viewed in good summer sunshine at around 1–2 p.m. GMT, 2–3 BST. Other stones with possible heads include Stones 23, 24, 28, 57, 58 and, at 7 a.m. and 5.30 p.m. BST, Stone 2.

This is creative stone imagery by the masters of the art of solar sculpture, in which the life of images is restricted to the interval when the sun is at the correct angle. Take

The face on Stone 53 is composed of a long straight nose and two natural holes as eyes.
Photographed 25 August, 3.00 p.m. BST, 2.00 GMT.

care, however, not to be deceived by the marks of lichen which occasionally create an eye where none should be. Lichen can mislead, and delight, with temporary images, as for instance with outer sarsen Stone 5 upon which, for ten years at least, the name DI has existed in yellow lichen in letters over a metre (three feet) high.

* * *

Before we leave Stonehenge, we need to examine, as we did at Avebury, what can be inferred about beliefs in creation mythology and its seasonal ritual, *the Marriage of the Gods*. There is good evidence for these at Stonehenge where the design plan indicates *a visual functioning of the Divine Marriage concept between as many as three different pairs of stones.*

The principal stone at Stonehenge, in its finished stage of construction, was not the Heel Stone but the vertical stone at the heart of the monument. This mica-filled megalith is best named the Goddess Stone. It was wrongly called the Altar Stone when it was thought that the builders' intention was to have it lie horizontally (it does so now only because it is crushed into the earth by the weight of megaliths on top of it). Apart from this, how many other stones are fundamental to the ritual working of Stonehenge?

A glance at a good plan of Stonehenge reveals that three stones were given special status—the only ones encircled by deep, large-diameter, narrowly-cut ditches, a practice clearly indicating an exceptional regard and devotion for them. One is the Heel Stone; the others are two of the four Station Stones.

The Station Stones are numbered 91, 92, 93 and 94. They lie on virtually the same circle as the Aubrey Holes, a little inside the monument's great circular ditch. Why were only two of the four stones, 92 and 94, chosen for this exceptional attention? The stones themselves are no longer there, having been demolished by robbers and souvenir and charm collectors, but the depth of the stone-holes (known for 92 and inferred for 94) indicate that the stones were big, and their large-diameter circles speak for their former size and importance.

Stones 91 and 93 survive, although they have fallen and been reduced in volume. Stone 93 is badly battered—a dismal relic of a once-special stone. But enough remains of Stone 91 to explain its choice. In its reduced state it is three metres (10 feet) long, but luckily it retains its natural feature, a deep groove along much of its length that is angled in the direction of Stone 92. Specialists in ancient religions, and practitioners of surviving pagan and Mother Earth religions (American Indians, Hindus, Tantrics, and others), recognise this as *a typical female stone*, if not a female-deity stone. This stone belongs to the same class as the deeply-grooved stone on Harestone Down above East Kennet and its long barrow.

The inter-relationships of the four stations provide a complete explanation for their

The dominant feature of Station Stone 91 is the deep, long groove which can be interpreted as yoni symbolism. When upright the shadow of Station Stone 92 used to fall upon it at midwinter sunset.

positions and probable shapes, because 92–91 and 94–93 are each arguably a male-female combination just as the Heel Stone and Altar Stone pair is.

The facts of trigonometry, accurate surveying and solar astronomy are undeniable. The position of encircled Stone 92 was such that at the midwinter sunset its shadow fell upon the grooved female Stone 91; whereas at the midsummer sunrise the shadow of encircled Stone 94 embraced Stone 93. This simple principle by which a shadow engulfs a second carefully placed stone parallels the situation at the South Circle of Avebury where it is known that a strong shadow from a phallic stone (the Obelisk) encounters a female stone—as with Stones 105 (at the summer sunrise) and 106 (at the Early-May Festival).

The Four-Stations arrangement at Stonehenge also includes the May-Festival sunset alignment. Indeed, the planning of the Four Stations probably began with it, as Norman Lockyer first explained a century ago. From the estimated centre of the monument the sunset was awaited on the eve of the May Festival, and this event decided

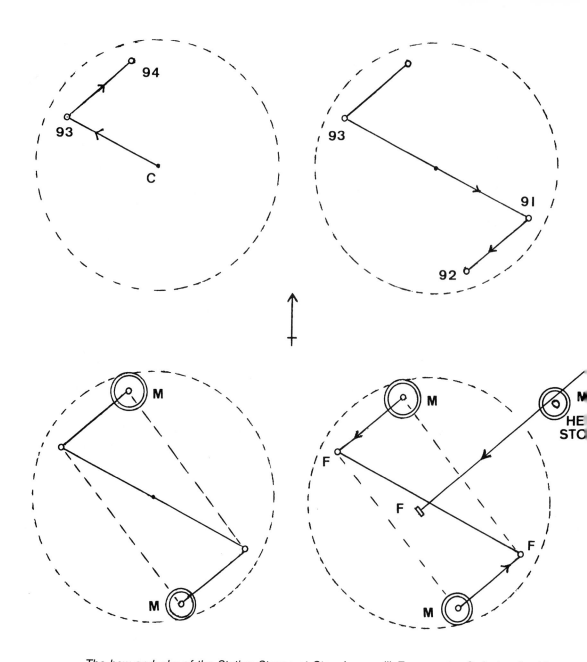

The how and why of the Station Stones at Stonehenge: (I) From centre C, facing the May-Festival Sunset, a female stone was erected at 93. From 93, in the direction of midsummer sunrise a male stone was erected at 94. (II) From 93, while facing the Early-February sunrise or Hallowe'en sunrise a female stone 91 was set up; this deeply-grooved stone is still present. From 91 in the direction of midwinter sunset a male stone was erected at 92. (III) By this means Sacred Marriage at the summer and winter solstices was effected between male (M) and female (F) stones, which may also explain why the male stones were provided with Tantric-type yoni rings. (IV) Fourthly came the building of the female stone circles, augmented by womb-shapes, to consummate marriage between a female focal stone F (the Altar Stone) and the sun/Heel Stone combination (M), for which purpose the Heel Stone was placed in eternal symbolic union with Earth at the centre of its own ring.

the position of Stone 93. A few weeks later the midsummer sunrise was sought. The skywatcher stood at the female Stone 93 and looked north-east; this decided the position of the male Stone 94. Once in place the shadow of Stone 94 would always meet Stone 93 at midsummer sunrise. *This was the first Sacred Marriage.*

In due course the early-February sunrise was attended, its direction being the opposite of the May Day sunset, for which purpose the observer looked from Stone 93 across the centre of Stonehenge. This decided where the grooved Stone 91 would go. Finally, from grooved Stone 91 the midwinter sunset was awaited, and this gave the position required for male Stone 92. For ever more, the shadow from Stone 92 would embrace the grooved Stone 91 at midwinter sunset—*and this was the second Sacred Marriage.* On this hypothesis the proposed phallic stones 92 and 94 were blessed with sacred circles, emphasising the esteem in which they were held.

The Sacred Marriage device was probably prepared for the Station Stones before the coming of the Welsh bluestones to the henge, and certainly before the arrival of the central sarsens from the Avebury Hills. When the bluestones started rising in the middle, the aim was to ensure that a few minutes after sunrise the externally-located Heel Stone, acting in its masculine capacity, would interact with the centrally positioned, mica-filled Goddess Stone or Altar Stone. This is *the third Sacred Marriage*, in recognition of which the Heel Stone was invested with a sacred circle of its own. A full account is given in *Stonehenge: The Secret of the Solstice.*

Not only does the Heel Stone serve as a phallic stone soon after the midsummer sunrise, but the Goddess Stone lies in the womb-cell at the focus of the bluestone circles and U-shapes. These settings suggest uterine femininity, standing for the Earth Mother herself. Such a tremendous effort later went into the building of sarsen Stonehenge that it seems the midsummer event there came to mean more to the believers than the earlier cosmic marriages between the outer pairs of Station Stones.

In short, I propose that the combined sarsen-bluestone monument was built as a high temple to the Earth Mother, complete with *garbha-grha* or womb-cell as in tens of thousands of Hindu temples, and for this purpose the Heel Stone functioned at the summer solstice as the Sky Father's member on earth. Maybe the Heel Stone was hermaphroditic, for there was divine triplicity too, as its three left-profile heads indicate. An earlier name for this stone than Friar's Heel may have been Freya's He-ol. Freya was a well-loved goddess in olden times, and the extreme antiquity of her origins is unknown. As pointed out by E. R. Rees, *Heol* is Welsh Celtic for track or way, and the Friar's Heel Stone stands at the entrance to the long Stonehenge Avenue.

In *Stonehenge: The Secret of the Solstice* I explained in detail how the Marriage of the Gods still takes place at Stonehenge at the midsummer solstice, 4,500 years after it was arranged to do so; and the photograph overleaf illustrates what Stonehenge looks like now when a full-size replica of the Goddess Stone is made to stand again. When

A replica of the Altar Stone or Goddess Stone, identical in height, width and thickness, stands in front of the fallen Altar Stone to demonstrate its relative size and position. The sun can never fully shine on it except at sunrise at the summer solstice, after which the shadow of the Heel Stone covers its bottom third.

freshly scraped and wetted, the Goddess Stone used to sparkle in the sunlight, like no other stone at Stonehenge.

The evidence suggests that both Avebury and Stonehenge were founded on the basis of firmly-held religious beliefs, and that much can still be learnt by studying the stones, their positions and individual shapes. Practically all the recent advances in this field have resulted from understanding the elements of the megalithic fertility religion and predicting the consequences.

17

THE GENIUS OF THE ANCIENT BRITONS

For miles around Avebury the chalkland of the Neolithic farmers was a sacred landscape through the middle of which flowed a sacred river fed by sacred springs—as it was at Stonehenge also.

Towards Avebury's hilly borders in the Early Neolithic Age, settlements, causewayed enclosures and long barrows appeared, and on the plain a thousand years later were constructed enduring temples and avenues of exceptional size and astonishing beauty. The inspiration was religious, linked in all probability to creation and fertility mythologies, and it ushered in an era of enchanting mystical art and stone sculpture.

William Stukeley was ahead of his time when he recognised Avebury for the outstanding temple that it is.

In 1743 he wrote: 'This temple, with the things belonging to it, when in perfection, must have been the work of a very great and learned people. The kind, manner, and idea of it, shews its extreme antiquity . . . The works themselves are an evidence of the genius of the founders.' They 'have a notorious grandeur of taste, a justness of plan, an apparent symmetry and a sufficient niceness in the execution' (*Abury:* 49).

Beyond megalithic Avebury over an area 'about four miles square' he appreciated the many manmade constructions in the landscape, like Silbury, the chambered barrows, and the lesser stone circles, and he was the first to state that all sixteen square miles were 'entirely sacred ground'.

Dr Stukeley went this far very well indeed. Given the limited knowledge of the times one can hardly blame him for crediting the history of the megaliths to the ancient order of Druids, although John Aubrey, half a century earlier, more astutely reckoned that it was safer to assign the origins of Avebury to the Ancient British rather than to the Druids.

William Stukeley's big mistake was to fantasise about biblical links between the Druids and the Old Testament Jews, and to identify the Avebury and Sanctuary circles and the attendant megalithic avenues with the symbolism of serpent fecundity and the God of the Christians.

'The wise Druids knew the internal meaning and purport of this great symbol of the fecundity of the deity . . . And never since the creation, was so magnificent an idea form'd in mortal minds, as this hieroglyphic here before us made in stone-work.' Dr Stukeley had devised a scheme by which the ancients succeeded in 'drawing down the blessings of divine providence upon that place and country, as it were, by sympathy and similitude' (*Abury:* 9).

Despite the literary inventions, and what Stukeley admitted to be speculations about the meaning of 'Abury and its parts' (*Abury:* 54), features with identifiable 'snake heads' were present all the while—although he never knew it because at least two of the three 'snake-heads' which are now visible were then hidden from sight. These heads are the left-profile ones on Stones 35, 68 and Z-stone v which simultaneously express the concept of a serpent and a 'Crone Goddess' or 'Wise Woman'.

These are just three examples from among some 60 henge or avenue stones which bear nearly-imperceptible artforms. For at Avebury the majority of surviving megaliths conceal skilfully-contrived sculptures in the form of human-head profiles or body parts, while the minority (like the Obelisk and Ring Stone) owe their presence to outline-shapes (phalluses, vulvas) or emplacements (circle centres, cove centres) which carried venerable symbolic meanings of their own. Although it was not a great accomplishment of civilisation like writing, it was an impressive cultural achievement.

The mystical conception and the artistic practice, based on the aim that sun and stone should function together, are straightforward. As the angle and direction of oblique solar rays change, the formless gathers form and images are tempted into being. Eventually an eye appears, upon which an ancestral spirit—the *manes*—or a deity might be considered active, until just as quickly the eye vanishes again. The climactic moment for public ceremony or private worship has gone.

Other examples have heads that are visible in profile at any time of day. For them it is the *angle* of view that matters, and often this is restricted. *Only* the viewer who knows how and where to look will see the image.

The concept is unique and awesome. It is an inconspicuous artform lost thousands of years ago when the race of artists disappeared from the face of the earth, along with the worshippers who understood and adored Avebury and Stonehenge. Some calamity, we know not what, intervened and the aged, ancestral fertility system collapsed. The megaliths were never used, never understood again.

Whereas just three surviving stones display left-profile snake-heads or Crone Goddess heads, several dozens more at Avebury exhibit other kinds of left-profile human head. Few have right-profile heads, and the reason has to do with the character of the fertility religion. Smaller objects have been found too, some carved, some natural but specially selected, and all displaying the same bias towards left-sidedness.

The people's belief-system shows every sign of incorporating ideas concerning the fertility deities Earth Mother and Sky Father. In early cultures fertility religions developed as a psychological response to the need to explain the world and its creation, and to control its excesses. This simple concept was widespread across the globe, and in one form or another was the foundation of the many pagan religions which later single-god religions suppressed.

At Avebury and Stonehenge the fertility concept was revealed by the layout of the stones. Avebury's stone circles express the notion of genital shrines of fertility and creation. At the South Circle the central male Obelisk served a sequence of female partners waiting round the perimeter, while at Stonehenge the layout more noticeably imitated the organs of generation of a female deity—that is, Goddess, Earth Goddess, or Earth Mother. At both temples the summer solstice event commemorated the creation of the world and ensured its perpetuation by re-enacting the Marriage of the Gods in a form the population could witness.

The sun's rays penetrate the Earth Mother's womb to arrive at a focal stone. This is the centre stone of the North Circle Cove at Avebury and it is the Goddess Stone at Stonehenge. The day is the summer solstice. At Avebury the solar-earth link is also achieved at the South Circle upon definite dates of the calendar, among which the celebration of the Early May Festival is pre-eminent. And lastly, there is the novel art-form—a species of sun-guided mobile sculpture—by which the movement of sun and shade over subtly-engraved stones brings the stones to life, seeming to animate them like spirits.

The explanation of Avebury and Stonehenge being the story of religion, Doctor William Stukeley has the last word: 'But those that approached this place with a purpose of religion, and that understood the mystical meaning thereof, must be extremely affected with it.' *Abury*, p. 49.

REFERENCES

ATKINSON, Richard (1968). Silbury Hill. *Antiquity*, vol. 42, 299; and (1969) vol. 43, 216.

AUBREY, John. *Monumenta Britannica*, vols. 1 and 2, published by J. Fowles and R. Legge in 1980. [Cathedral 21; south entrance stone, 37; stone burning 38].

BARKER, C. T. (1984). The long mounds of the Avebury Region. *Wilts. Arch. Mag.*, vol. 79, 7–38.

BARKER, C., T. (1984). Millbarrow and Shelving Stone—finally laid to rest? *Wilts. Arch. Mag.*, vol. 78, 115–17.

BARNATT, John (1989). *Stone Circles of Britain* part 2. Oxford BAR British Series, Oxford [Winterbourne Bassett 452; Beckhampton Penning 505; Langdean 505].

BENTNALL, H. C. (1946). Sarsens. *Wilts. Arch. Mag.*, vol. 51, 419–39 (p. 426).

BURL, H. A. W. (1976). *Stone Circles of the British Isles*. Yale [Langdean 317, 348].

BURL, H. A. W. (1979). *Prehistoric Avebury*. Yale, New Haven and London. [Cove and northerly moonrise 158, 218; rites with bones at coves 163, 218; night rituals 218].

BURL, H. A. W. (1988). Coves: Structural enigmas of the Neolithic. *Wilts. Arch. Mag.*, vol. 82, 1–18.

CLEAL, R. J. M., WALKER, K. E. and MONTAGUE, R. (1995). *Stonehenge in its Landscape*. English Heritage, London.

CRAWFORD, O. G. S. (1922). Notes on field-work round Avebury, December 1921. *Wilts Arch. Mag.*, vol. 42, 52–63.

CRAWFORD, O. G. S. and KEILLER, A. (1928). *Wessex from the Air*. Oxford [213].

CUNNINGTON, Maud E. (1913a). The re-erection of two fallen stones and the discovery of an interment with drinking cup at Avebury. *Wilts. Arch. Mag.*, vol. 38, 1–8.

CUNNINGTON, Maud E. (1913b). A buried stone in the Kennet Avenue. *Wilts. Arch. Mag.*, vol. 37, 12–14.

CUNNINGTON, Maud E. (1932). The Sanctuary on Overton Hill, near Avebury. *Wilts. Arch. Mag.*, vol. 45, 300–35 [303].

CYRIAX, Tony (1921). Ancient burial places. *Antiq. J.*, vol. 28.

DAMES, Michael (1976). *The Silbury Treasure*. Thames & Hudson, London.

DAMES, Michael (1977). *The Avebury Cycle*. Thames & Hudson, London. [Stone 44 at Kennet long barrow 58–9; Stone 35a 94–6;

moon and Kennet Avenue 100; Wedding rite 154–5].

DEVEREUX, Paul (1992). *Symbolic Landscapes*. Gothic Image, Glastonbury [151–3].

DURDIN-ROBERTSON, Lawrence (1990). *The Year of the Goddess*. Antiquarian Press (refers on p. 41 to Morgan, *Matriarchy News*, no. 2).

ELIADE, M. (1958). *Patterns in Comparative Religion*. Sheed & Ward, London.

FERGUSSON, James (1860). *Stonehenge Quarterly Review*, no. 108, 200–25.

FOWLES, John and LEGG, Rodney (eds.), 1980, 1982. *John Aubrey's Monumenta Britannica*. (Sherborne, Dorset).

GIMBUTAS, M. (1989). *The Language of the Megaliths*. Harper & Row, San Francisco; Thames & Hudson, London.

GIMBUTAS, Marija (1991). *The Civilisation of the Goddess*. Harper & Row, San Francisco.

GRAY, H. St. G. (1935). The Avebury excavations 1908–1922. *Archaeologia*, vol. 84, 99–162.

GRINSELL, L. V. (1937). *Folklore*, vol. 48, 245–56.

GRINSELL, L. V. (1957). Victoria County History of Wiltshire, vol. 1, 125 [Beckhampton Penning stones 3; Langdean 67].

GRINSELL, L. V. (1976). *Folklore of Ancient Sites in Britain*. David & Charles, Newton Abbott.

HUNTER, J. (1829). The present state of Avebury, Wilts. *Gentleman's Magazine*, 1829, Part II, 1–7.

KEILLER, A. and PIGGOTT, S. (1936). The West Kennet Avenue: Excavations, 1934–35. *Antiquity*, vol. 10, 417–27 [420].

KEILLER, A. (1939). Avebury: Summary of excavations 1937 and 1938. *Antiquity*, vol. 13, 223–33.

KEMPSON, E. G. H. (1955). The Anglo-Saxon name for the Avebury Circle. *Wilts. Arch. Mag.*, vol. 56, 60–1; 190.

KING, B. (1879). Avebury. The Beckhampton Avenue. *Wilts. Arch. Mag.*, vol. 18, 377–83.

KNIGHT, Peter (1998). *Sacred Dorset*. Capall Bann, Chieveley, Berkshire.

LOCKYER, Norman (1909). *Stonehenge and Other British Monuments*. Macmillan, London [May Eve sunset 88–95; Devil's Den 337–9].

LONG, William (1858). Abury. *Wilts. Arch. Mag.*, vol. 4, 309–63 (Falkners circle 345).

LONG, William (1878). Abury notes. *Wilts. Arch. Mag.*, vol. 17, 327–35.

LUKIS, W. C. (1883). Report on the prehistoric monuments of Wiltshire, Somerset and South Wales. *Proc. Soc. Antiq. London*, vol. 9, 344–55 [347].

MACKIE, Euan W. (1997). Maeshowe and the winter solstice. *Antiquity*, vol. 71, 338–59.

MALONE, Caroline (1989). *Avebury*. Batsford, London.

MEADEN, G. T. (1991). *The Goddess of the Stones*. Souvenir Press, London.

MEADEN, G. T. (1992). *The Stonehenge Solution*. Souvenir Press, London.

MEADEN, G. T. (1997). *Stonehenge: The Secret of the Solstice*. Souvenir Press, London.

MEADEN, G. T. (1997). The stone circle near Winterbourne Bassett. *3rd Stone*, Devizes, no. 25, 20–1.

MEREWETHER, John (1851). Diary of the examination of barrows and other earthworks in the neighbourhood of Silbury Hill, Wiltshire in July and August 1849. *Proc. Archaeol. Institute (Salisbury volume)*, 82–107.

MEYRICK, O. (1955). The Broadstones (Clatford). *Wilts. Arch. Mag.*, vol. 56, 192–3.

MEYRICK. O. (1959). An early eighteenth-century visitor to Avebury. *Wilts. Arch. Mag.*, vol. 57, 225–6.

MORTIMER, Neil (1997). On longan dene neodewearde (Langdean). *3rd Stone*, Devizes, no. 26, 24–6.

MORTIMER, Neil (1998). Beckhampton Penning. *3rd Stone*, Devizes, no. 29, 17–18.

PARKER PEARSON, M. and RAMILISONINA (1998). Stonehenge for the ancestors. *Antiquity*, vol. 72, 308–26.

PASSMORE, A. D. (1922). The Devil's Den

Dolmen, Clatford Bottom. *Wilts. Arch. Mag.*, vol. 41, 523–30.

PASSMORE, A. D. (1926a). Avebury—A new stone in the Kennet Avenue. *Wilts. Arch. Mag.*, vol. 43, 341–3.

PASSMORE, A. D. (1926b). *Wilts. Arch. Mag.*, vol. 43, 364–5, with photograph and plan on plate between.

PIGGOTT, Stuart (1940). Timber circles: a re-examination. *Arch. J.*, vol. 96, 193–222.

PIGGOTT, Stuart (1946). The destruction of The Sanctuary on Overton Hill. *Wilts. Arch. Mag.*, vol. 51, 470–1.

PIGGOTT, Stuart (1962). *The West Kennet Long Barrow Excavations 1955–56.* H.M.S.O., London.

PITTS, M. and WHITTLE, A. (1992). The development and date of Avebury. *Proc. Prehistoric Soc.*, vol. 58, 203–12.

POLLACK, Rachel (1997). *The Body of the Goddess.* Element Books, Shaftesbury, Dorset, and Rockport, Mass.

POLLARD, Joshua (1992). The Sanctuary, Overton Hill, Wiltshire: A Re-examination. *Proc. Prehistoric. Soc.*, vol. 58, 213–26.

RUDGELEY, Richard (1998). *Lost Civilisations of the Stone Age.* Century, London.

SMITH, A. C. (1867). Excavations at Avebury. *Wilts. Arch. Mag.*, vol. 10, 209–16.

SMITH, A. C. (1885) *Guide to the British and Roman antiquities of the North Wiltshire Down in a hundred square miles around Avebury.* Map, second edition, Devizes.

SMITH, Isobel (1964). Avebury: The Northern Inner Circle. *Wilts. Arch. Mag.*, vol. 59, 181.

SMITH, Isobel (1965). *Windmill Hill and Avebury: Excavations by Alexander Keiller 1925–1939.* Oxford University Press. [Barber's coins 177–9, Edict of Nantes 179; gender of stones 197, 251; inner North Circle 223; prosperous society 253].

STRAFFON, Cheryl (1997). *The Earth Goddess*, p. 53, Blandford, London.

STUKELEY, W. (1722–24a). *The history of the temples of the ancient Celts.* Unpublished (Bodleian Library, Oxford, MS Eng. Misc.

c.323), (quoted by Ucko *et al.*, p.279 *loc. cit.*).

STUKELEY, William (1722–24b). *Celtic religion.* unpubl. Central Cardiff Library (quoted by Ucko *et al.*, p.76 *loc. cit.*).

STUKELEY, William (1722). *Itinerarium Curiosum* Pt 1, 132. Centuria, London.

STUKELEY, William (1743). *Abury.* London.

THOMAS, Julian and WHITTLE, Alasdair (1986). Anatomy of a tomb—West Kennet revisited. *Oxford Journal of Archaeology*, vol. 5, 127–56.

THOMAS, Nicholas (1952). A Neolithic chalk cup from Wilsford in the Devizes Museum, and notes on others. *Wilts. Arch. Mag.*, vol. 54, 451–62.

THOMAS, Nicholas (1957). A Neolithic pit on Waden Hill. *Wilts. Arch. Mag.*, vol. 64, 167–71.

THURNAM, John (1861). Examination of a chambered long barrow at West Kennet, Wiltshire. *Archaeologia*, vol. 38, 405–21.

TWINING, Thomas (1723). *Avebury in Wiltshire, the remains of a Roman work.*

UCKO, Peter J., HUNTER, Michael, CLARK, Alan J. and DAVID, Andrew (1991). *Avebury Reconsidered.* Unwin Hyman, London.

VATCHER, Faith de M. (1969). Avebury: Beckhampton Avenue. *Wilts. Arch. Mag.*, vol. 64, 127.

WALKER, Barbara (1983). *The Woman's Encyclopaedia of Myths and Secrets.* Harper & Row, San Francisco [Tara 976].

WHITTLE, Alasdair (1994). Excavations at Millbarrow chambered tomb, Winterbourne Monkton. *Wilts. Arch. Mag.*, vol. 87, 1–53.

WHITTLE, Alasdair (1997). *Sacred Mound and Holy Rings.* Oxbow Books, Oxford [meaning of Silbury and the rings 164–7].

YOUNG, W. E. V. (1949). A Beaker interment at Beckhampton. *Wilts. Arch. Mag.*, vol. 53, 311–27.

YOUNG, W. E. V. (1959). The West Kennet Avenue. *Wilts. Arch. Mag.*, vol. 57, 229–30.

YOUNG, W. E. V. (1961). The West Kennet Avenue. *Wilts. Arch. Mag.*, vol. 58, 30.

INDEX